EARNING FREEDOM
CONQUERING A 45-YEAR PRISON TERM
Michael G. Santos

PRISON! 8,344TH DAY
Typical Day in an Ongoing Journey
Michael G. Santos

HOW TO EARN MILLIONS $$$
SUCCESS! AFTER PRISON
Michael G. Santos

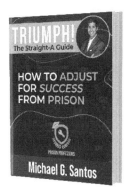

TRIUMPH!
The Straight-A Guide
HOW TO ADJUST FOR SUCCESS FROM PRISON
Michael G. Santos

TEN STEPS
Introductory Course
Prepare for Success from Prison
Michael G. Santos

REENTRY PREPARATION
Personal Leadership Series: 1
Be the CEO of Your Life
Bill McGlashan

REENTRY PREPARATION
Personal Leadership Series: 2
Be the CEO of Your Life
Mossimo Giannulli

REENTRY PREPARATION
Personal Leadership Series: 4
Be the CEO of Your Life
Michael G. Santos

REENTRY PREPARATION
Personal Leadership Series: 3
Be the CEO of Your Life
Dr. Jeffrey Gallups

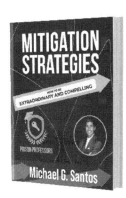

MITIGATION STRATEGIES
HOW TO BE EXTRAORDINARY AND COMPELLING
Michael G. Santos

EARNING FREEDOM
CONQUERING A 45-YEAR PRISON TERM
Michael G. Santos

JOURNAL & LESSONS DAILY
Version 1—2022
Michael G. Santos

With Gratitude to our Sponsors

TESTIMONIALS

I regard Michael Santos as an eminent policy analyst in the field of sentencing and corrections. At Stanford Law School, we welcome his great wisdom about the most needed and feasible improvements in reentry practice and programs.

Joan Petersilia, Professor of Law,
Stanford Law School

As Deputy Warden of Programs and Services at the Maine State Prison I wanted to find a Reentry program designed specifically to build intrinsic motivation for people in prison. I personally facilitate the Mastermind course to our prison's most problematic prisoners. This strategy keeps the highly resistant participant engaged and challenged.

Michael Tausek, Deputy Warden
Maine State Prison

Prisons should give serious consideration to the curriculum prepared by Michael Santos, specifically designed to prepare inmates for release. I read his book, Earning Freedom: Conquering a 45-Year Prison Term. He has the life experience, knowledge, skills, and intellect to contribute to the rehabilitation process.

Honorable Robert Tafoya,
Superior Court Judge,
Bakersfield, California

Michael Santos is a great resource for students at UC Berkeley! I invite him to speak regularly to my large class in Wheeler Hall, with more than 500 students in attendance each time. His dynamic presentations always inspire and educate the Berkeley community. Michael shows the power of human potential and we welcome him to present at Berkeley anytime.

Professor Alan Ross,
UC Berkeley Haas Business School

I've done business with Michael Santos and I will continue to do business with Michael Santos. He inspires me every day and I'm glad to have his friendship. I've never had any doubt of the success he would build.

Lee Nobmann,
Founder, Golden State Lumber

Michael Santos wants to give back. I find him to be very genuine. He feels very strongly that whatever he can do to help offenders change their lives and become successful, he would like to do. It's a very compelling story.

Michael Colwell,
Assistant Director
Washington State Correctional Industries

Immediately after his release in 2013, Santos began lecturing at a respected state university. Today, he has a website, course materials for persons facing lengthy prison sentences, scores of supporters and mentors, and the charisma and character to hold a law symposium audience spellbound for every minute of his thirty-minute presentation.

Rory Little,
Professor of Law, University of California Hastings College of the Law

Michael Santos is one of the most inspiring people that I have ever met. I had the good fortune of meeting him last year when he spoke at Gideon's Promise. He has inspired many lawyers. He works with lawyers to improve the outcome for our clients, preparing them so they have meaningful lives in prison and beyond.

Colette Tvedt, Director,
National Association of Criminal Defense Lawyers

Michael Santos has channeled his fine mind and abundant energy into academic work of excellent quality. His personal and academic achievements while incarcerated convince me that he has become a serious and intellectually sophisticated man who has great potential for doing good as well as doing well. His life and skills give promise to anyone enduring challenge.

Alfred Cohn,
Professor of Psychology,
Hofstra University

Michael Santos' articles have appeared in scholarly journals and textbooks. His knowledge of the federal prison system and succeeding inside and outside of prison is without equal.

George F. Cole,
Professor Emeritus,
University of Connecticut

I have noticed over the years that we listen to some people because of what they have to say, and that we listen to others because of where they have been. I listen to Michael Santos for both reasons.

J. Colin Harris,
Professor of Religion of and Philosophy
Mercer University

"Santos relates how he has structured his prison time to avoid confrontations with other inmates and trouble with guards and has pursued every educational opportunity open to him. This culminated in a master's degree from Hofstra University."

Edward Humes,
Los Angeles Times Sunday Book Review

As Success After Prison shows, nothing can stop an individual who chooses to success. Despite being incarcerated for longer than 26 years, Michael Santos has come back to society strong. He quickly began applying all that he learned to launch a number of successful business ventures while simultaneously making contributions to society.

Tim Ufkes,
Managing Director
Berkadia

In Success After Prison, Michael Santos shows the results of making good decisions. Even though he started life with a 45-year prison term, he came out and quickly launched a career that brought him into the top percentile of all earners. He embodies the characteristics of a hardcore closer. If you follow the guidance in Success After Prison, you will too!

Ryan Stewman,
Hardcore Closer

I was happy to assist Michael with the purchase of three investment properties. I found him to be honest and fully capable of articulating an investment strategy—just as he described in Success After Prison. I'm looking forward to assisting Michael with all of his real estate financing needs. His work ethic, as characterized in this book, inspires me to work toward achieving more.

Derek Clemons, Mortgage Banker,
Evergreen Mortgage

Other Books by
Michael G. Santos / Prison Professors

Earning Freedom:
Conquering a 45-Year Prison Term
PrisonProfessors.com
(Shows strategies to build strength and discipline through long term)

Prison! My 8,344th Day
PrisonProfessors.com
(Shows strategies to be productive through single day in prison)

Triumph! The Straight-A Guide
Preparing Prisoners for Reentry
PrisonProfessors.com
(Shows strategies to serve time productively)

Success After Prison
How I Built Assets Worth $1,000,000
After Being Released from Prison
PrisonProfessors.com
(Shows outcomes for people who use time in prison to prepare for success)

Ten Steps to Prepare for Success
from Jail or Prison
PrisonProfessors.com
(Self-directed course to help people in jail or prison)

Inside: Life Behind Bars in America
St. Martin's Press
(Insight to high-security prisons in America)

Success After Prison
ISBN: 9798364801869

To Contact us—Please visit:
www.PrisonProfessors.com

To get our newsletter: Send invite to
Impact@PrisonProfessors.com

Dear Course Participant:

Our team at Prison Professors will work hard to prove worthy of your trust. We produced this self-directed course, Preparing for Success after Prison, hoping to improve outcomes for all justice-impacted people.

My name is Michael Santos. In 1987, I began a 26-year odyssey through the Bureau of Prisons. At the start, I only wanted to get out. Then, after a jury convicted me and I faced a sentence of life without parole, I realized I would have to make changes.

After reading a story about Socrates, I learned that change began with introspection. It also required that I start thinking about the best possible outcome. In this 10-module course, I share what I learned from leaders.

While working through this program, please consider helping our efforts to improve outcomes for people in prison. We strive to help legislators, policymakers, and citizens understand the value of incentivizing a pursuit of excellence. We'd like to see reforms that offer more mechanisms that would encourage people to work toward earning freedom. You'll see that message throughout this course.

To become more successful at influencing positive reforms, we ask for your help. Legislators would be more inclined to listen to the need for meaningful reforms if we could show that participants in our classes:

» Participate in other classes that lead to success after prison,
» Avoid disciplinary infractions,
» Build positive mentor relationships, and
» Memorialize their journey.

We will do our part to prove worthy of your support. Still, we ask participants to do their part and work through this course with an open mind and understanding of their role in influencing positive reforms that will improve the lives of all justice-impacted people.

Respectfully,
Michael Santos
www.PrisonProfessors.com / PSAP@PrisonProfessors.com

Contents

1. Introduction

WHY I WROTE SUCCESS AFTER PRISON

Success after prison becomes more likely when a person lays out a plan at the start of the journey. In this section, I strive to show the strategies that I used to make it through 26 years.

My name is Michael Santos. I'm striving to write this book in a conversational style, hoping to convey messages that leaders taught me while I climbed through 9,500 days in prison. Their lessons influenced my adjustment. During the quarter century that I served, I spent time in federal prisons of:

1. High security,
2. Medium security,
3. Low security,
4. Minimum security

Then, on August 13, 2012, I transitioned to a halfway house in the Tenderloin District of San Francisco. And in February 2013, I transitioned to home confinement. On August 12, 2013, I concluded my obligation to the Federal Bureau of Prisons.

But I wasn't finished with the system.

The crimes that led me to prison related to trafficking cocaine. Following a jury trial, US District Court Judge Jack Tanner sentenced me to serve a 45-year sentence. Since the crimes occurred before November 1, 1987, he did not rely upon the Federal Sentencing Guidelines. The sentencing laws allowed me to earn credit for avoiding disciplinary infractions. Since I earned all the statutory "good time" credits possible, I finished my sentence with the Bureau of Prisons after 26 years rather than 45.

Once I finished with the Bureau of Prisons, however, other jurisdictions had control of my liberty. First, I would have to conclude seven years with Federal Probation for Supervised Release. Once I finished Supervised Release with US Probation, I would go through 19 years on parole with the US Parole Commission. And after the 19 years of parole, the sentence required that I serve an additional three years of Special Parole.

Obligations to US Probation and the US Parole Commission did not prove to be a problem. Once authorities allowed me to walk out of the federal prison in Atwater and I met my wife, Carole, in the lobby, I appreciated the liberty. Since we'd married inside a federal prison, I looked forward to building my life with her.

This book isn't about prison. Instead, it will show how earlier decisions led to opportunities for success upon release. I publish this book as part of a series, including:

» Earning Freedom: Conquering a 45-Year Prison Term

◊ In *Earning Freedom*, I reveal the strategies and tactics that guided my adjustment through prisons of every security level. Readers will learn how every decision in prison relates to prospects for success after release.

» Prison! My 8,344th Day—A Typical Day in an Ongoing Journey

◊ In *Prison! My 8,344th Day*, readers learn how to maintain discipline through a single day. Opportunity costs accompany every decision we make.

I wrote the two earlier books during my final years of imprisonment. For decades I'd been preparing for my release. As the date got closer, I wanted to create resources that would allow me to build a career around all that I learned. Those two books, in my view, would show people how to maintain hope while growing through multiple decades or single days.

In *Success after Prison*, I wanted to create a new resource. It would show people the relationship between a person's decisions while incarcerated and the opportunities that open upon release.

We all face struggles or challenges at some point in life. When we go through those challenges, they can obliterate hope. Since leaders taught me, I feel a duty and

responsibility to share what I learned through the long odyssey in the criminal justice system.

Anyone can use the same strategies that empowered me to conquer struggle. I'm sure of it. Before I get into the strategy, let me explain why I initially wrote this book and why I am rewriting (and recording) the manuscript in the fall of 2022.

SOME BACKSTORY:

Judge Charles Pyle, a federal judge from Arizona, reached out to me in early 2015. I didn't know Judge Pyle. He had heard about my journey and my work to improve outcomes for justice-impacted people.

What is a justice-impacted person?

From my perspective, a justice-impacted person includes every person who:

» has gone through any phase of the system,
» works in the system, and
» supports people in the criminal justice system.

I work to improve outcomes for those people.

Judge Pyle and his team were coordinating a judicial conference for practitioners in the Ninth Circuit of the US judicial system. The audience would include more than 1,000 people, including judges, directors of prison systems, wardens, and those who worked in reentry programs. Judge Pyle asked if I would attend the conference as a keynote speaker.

Since concluding my obligation to the Bureau of Prisons, I've spoken for audiences across the United States. Sometimes those events paid me well. Other times I volunteered to present without compensation. I believe in the cause of working to improve the outcomes of America's criminal justice system.

On a previous occasion, while still confined to the halfway house, judges from the Southern District of California invited me to make a presentation. Those judges wanted me to address what happens after a judge sentences a person to the custody of the attorney general.

After many challenges from the halfway house, leaders in the regional office of the BOP authorized me to fly from San Francisco to San Diego. After listening to representatives from the Bureau of Prisons tell their stories, I got to offer the judges a different perspective.

With the invitation from Judge Pyle, I had a second opportunity to influence judges. Regardless of what business I'm building, I welcome every opportunity to advocate for justice-impacted people. That means striving to help decision-makers understand steps we can take to improve the outcomes of the system.

I looked forward to the three-day event in the fall of 2015. Judge Pyle told me that Paul Wright, another formerly incarcerated person, would also present as a speaker. While I served my sentence, I read about Paul's work.

Paul Wright started the award-winning newspaper *Prison Legal News* while he served a lengthy sentence in Washington State's prison system. Although I'd never met Paul previously, his work inspired me for many years.

In *Prison Legal News,* readers can learn about case law relating to people in prison. The newspaper published commentaries, essays, and perceptions about what people would experience in jails and prisons worldwide.

Over the years, Paul grew the distribution of his influential magazine. His subscription base grew across the nation. Paul put a team together in the community. They took pains to print the magazine and mail copies to each subscriber.

Many administrators resisted *Prison Legal News*, and I know that he paid a heavy price for his commitment to publishing. In addition to the newspaper, Paul authored several books. Since his work inspired me over the decades I served, I looked forward to meeting him at the Sacramento judicial conference.

Once I got there, Paul and I walked to a restaurant after the first day of the conference. We conversed while eating at a seafood restaurant. During the conversation, I learned more about Paul's commitment to helping people in prison. *Prison Legal News*, he said, reached more than 200,000 people each month. He suggested

that I purchase advertising space to reach more people who might have an interest in the books I wrote.

Before that conversation, I had never considered purchasing advertising for books. I wrote several books during the 26 years that I served. Initially, I worked with publishers that had marketing departments. They controlled the distribution of the books through their end-user sales force or their distributors. Publishers coordinated reviews that made book buyers aware of the various titles that I wrote.

Later, with the advancement of the internet, publishing my books became more efficient. The distribution came through various channels, which I'll describe in the following chapters. Advertising to a mass audience hadn't been one of my strategies. I asked Paul more about the process and the readership.

Prison Legal News reaches prisoners in every state, he explained. In addition to the newspaper that went into prisons, his website reached a broad audience of lawyers and others who expressed interest in prisons.

Since I wanted to support his team's effort with *Prison Legal News*, and he convinced me that I could reach more readers, I decided to advertise with him.

My conversation with Paul inspired me to write a new book that could influence people's adjustment in prison. They needed hope. During the 26 months that had passed since I finished my sentence with the BOP, I'd built an asset portfolio worth more than $1,000,000. Had I still been in prison, I would have liked to read a book that showed how decisions inside influenced opportunities outside.

Few people would expect opportunities to open for a person that served multiple decades in prison. Part of my advocacy work focuses on showing more people how to come out of prison strong, with their dignity intact. With that end in mind, I made a commitment to start writing *Success after Prison*.

Writing became essential to my release-preparation strategy from the earliest part of my journey. Besides authoring books that I would publish under my name, I became a ghostwriter for other people while I served my sentence. The chapters that follow offer more details on that adjustment strategy.

Since I didn't have access to technology, I wrote each manuscript in longhand. After writing, I would send the manuscripts home. My wife, Carole, would convert my handwritten pages into a digital format. She printed the pages, then sent them to my prison for editing. We devoted hundreds of hours to that process of writing, editing, and rewriting until we published the paperback books.

I may not win writing awards or earn distinction for eloquence through these projects. I have different intentions. I want to build hope for justice-impacted people. If they adhere to the same path that leaders taught me, they will restore confidence and strength while climbing through imprisonment.

What's the path?

It's simple. Leaders teach that anyone who wants to overcome a challenge should adhere to the following strategy:

1. Start by defining success,
2. Create a plan that will make incremental advancements,
3. Put priorities in place,
4. Develop tools, tactics, and resources,
5. Execute the plan with clear accountability metrics.

Following my presentation at the judicial conference where I met Paul, opportunities opened for me to reach more justice-impacted people. A US Attorney—Alicia Limtiaco—invited me to create a series of presentations for her district. Then, I spoke with Andre Matevousian, who served as the warden of a federal prison in Atwater, California.

The following pages reveal more about how interactions from that judicial conference opened opportunities to make a more significant impact on improving outcomes for justice-impacted people. They also pushed me to accelerate the time and energy I intended to write *Success after Prison*.

I finished the first version of this manuscript on December 4, 2015, approximately 28 months after finishing my obligation to the Bureau of Prisons. With this revised draft, which I'm publishing in November 2022, I'll include an epilogue to share more about how adjustment patterns in prison influence prospects for success upon release.

If I've done my job, readers will understand more about why it's never too early, and it's never too late to begin working toward a better outcome.

SELF-DIRECTED QUESTIONS:

In the pages to follow, to complete a self-directed exercise, write your responses to the following three questions.

1. In what ways are you preparing for success upon release?

2. How do your earlier decisions relate to the activities you're pursuing today?

3. How would you define success upon release?

2. The Beginnings
FINDING AVATARS TO GUIDE ADJUSTMENTS

SOCRATES AND SUCCESS

If we're losing hope from the challenges we face, Socratic questioning can help us find our way. What would our avatars expect?

I'm typing this manuscript on a fabulous iMac computer. When I served my sentence, I had to write manuscripts by hand. Since getting out, I've become addicted to technology products by Apple, Microsoft, Adobe, and Google. I use them every day. These tools allow me to write more efficiently and become more productive.

Institutions control people's time while they serve sentences, but people must work productively once they get out. Employers resist hiring people who do not know how to use technology.

The internet didn't exist when I started serving my sentence. Until I got out, I never sent an email, used a smartphone, or made a video. My wife got me a MacBook Pro within days of getting out, and I began training. Although I didn't get to use computers while I served my sentence, the books I read and the courses I took inside positioned me to learn quickly once I got out.

I started typing the first version of this manuscript on Saturday morning, December 4, 2015. I aimed to complete the manuscript and publish the book before the new year. To reach that goal, I would have to apply myself. I didn't want to squander an opportunity that opened to connect with people serving time.

Warden Andre Matevousian invited me to make a presentation at the United States Penitentiary in Atwater on January 8, 2016. Before I got there, I wanted to write a book to help people inside see how their decisions could lead to success upon release. I knew that staff members and other leaders tried to convey that message. Somehow, I thought the men would find more meaning in the message if they heard it from a person who went through prison and returned to society.

The Warden asked me to talk with the men about the importance of setting clear goals. Since I never asked anyone to do anything I didn't do, I set a goal. I would write the manuscript, publish the book, and show the tools I created to hold myself accountable. People in prison should see how small and incremental steps lead to bigger goals that can open new opportunities.

While incarcerated, I learned the power of seeing far into the future. I would need to use time wisely to build the future I wanted. Every decision came with an opportunity cost. Decisions would either move me closer to success or complicate my life in ways that could lead to more problems.

The roots of my invitation to speak at USP Atwater began many years earlier. In many ways, I would argue that I started sowing the seeds for that invitation back in 1987 while I was locked inside the Pierce County Jail, waiting for sentencing. I read a book about Socrates, and he inspired my adjustment through prison. Instead of dwelling on the problems I created for myself, Socrates taught me to start thinking about the future I wanted to build. That book influenced the decisions I made in prison.

My adjustment influenced my transfer to the federal prison in Lompoc in 2004, during my 17th year of imprisonment. When I got there, Andre Matevousian served as the Captain at Lompoc, meaning he led the custody and security staff.

While I was in Lompoc, *The Los Angeles Times* published a review for my book *Inside: Life Behind Bars in America.* When a correctional officer saw the review, he cited me with a disciplinary infraction for "running a business." He led me into the Special Housing Unit, and from there, I began using the administrative remedy process to contest the appropriateness of the disciplinary infraction. Through that experience, I got to know Captain Matevousian. After the region agreed to expunge the rule violation, administrators ordered my transfer from Lompoc to a camp in Taft, California.

I didn't see Warden Matevousian again until 2015, following my luncheon keynote speech at the judicial conference in Sacramento. Warden Matevousian approached and congratulated me for the career I had built since getting out. He extended an open invitation to visit Atwater—the prison that released me in 2013—so I could meet his team and speak to the people inside.

I welcomed the opportunity.

Since concluding my journey as federal prisoner number 16377-004, I've worked to build a career around all that I learned. To provide some context, I owe readers at least an abbreviated background.

Those who've read my earlier books, particularly *Earning Freedom: Conquering a 45-Year Prison Term*, won't learn anything new in this chapter. I won't take the time to provide the same level of detail I wrote in that comprehensive book. For those who have not read *Earning Freedom* but want a wider glimpse of my prison journey, visit www.PrisonProfessors.com to get a digital copy of *Earning Freedom*. Libraries may offer copies of the paperback or audio version.

After this initial chapter, the remaining chapters of *Success after Prison* will show how decisions in prison relate to opportunities that opened since my release. We'll start with the backstory.

BACKSTORY:

In 1982, I graduated from Shorecrest High School in Seattle as a mediocre student. Immediately following graduation, I started working in a contracting company my father began during my childhood.

My father escaped from Cuba and worked hard with my mother to build his company. He hoped to pass the business along to me after I matured, but I disappointed my mom and dad during my reckless adolescence.

When I was 20, in 1984, I saw the movie *Scarface* with Al Pacino. Pacino played the character Tony Montana, a cool Cuban immigrant who built a fortune trafficking cocaine. Rather than following in my father's footsteps, I made the bad decision to follow guidance from Tony Montana.

Tony said, "In this country, first you get the money, then you get the power, then you get the woman."

From my immature perspective, I admired Tony's philosophy. As the film's closing scenes depicted, his outlook on life didn't work out so well.

Nevertheless, after watching the film, I coordinated a scheme to earn quick money by distributing cocaine. Foolishly, I believed that I could shield myself from prosecution. By limiting my role to negotiating transactions and hiring other people to transport the cocaine or storing the cocaine, I convinced myself that I could avoid the criminal justice system.

On August 11, 1987, I learned how badly I had misinterpreted the criminal justice system. In the late afternoon, I saw three DEA agents pointing guns at my head. They ordered me to put my hands up, searched me, and as they locked my wrists in steel cuffs behind my back, they let me know of their warrant for my arrest.

My odyssey through the criminal justice began. When I refer to the journey as an "odyssey," I allude to Homer's classic Greek mythology. Homer wrote about Odysseus, who had gone on a long journey to fight a war. He had to endure many trials and tribulations before returning home.

Over the decades that followed my arrest, I'd go through the following:

» Federal holding centers,
» Court proceedings,
» Jails,
» Federal transit centers,
» Many Prisons,
» Halfway house,
» Supervised Release,
» Parole, and
» Special parole.

The following pages tell the story of how decisions I made inside influenced my life outside. I hope this message inspires other justice-impacted people to prepare for their odyssey and successful outcome.

TRANSFORMATION AFTER TRIAL

Wanting nothing more than to get out of jail, I welcomed the optimism I heard from my attorney after the arrest. When he told me that a significant difference existed between an indictment and a conviction, I put my future in his hands.

Then I proceeded to make every wrong decision a defendant could make:

» I refused to accept responsibility.
» I didn't contemplate expressing remorse.
» While in custody, I stayed involved with the criminal enterprise I had begun.
» I took the witness stand to testify during my trial and lied to the jury.

Members of the jury saw through my perjury and convicted me of every count.

A NEW PHILOSOPHY:

After the jury convicted me, the US Marshals returned me to the Pierce County Jail. While in my cell, I came to terms with the bad decisions I had made for the first time. I began to pray for guidance. Those prayers led me to a philosophy book, and I came across the story of Socrates.

At that time, I didn't know anything about philosophy or Socrates. While reading the early chapters, I learned that he served ancient Athens as a teacher. Laws of that era criminalized the ruling class from teaching people of lower classes.

Socrates broke that law. He believed that every human being had a right to learn. Authorities arrested him and put him on trial for violating the law. Following his conviction, the judges sentenced him to death. They ordered jailers to confine him until his execution date.

While waiting for authorities to carry out his death, Crito, a friend of Socrates, visited him in jail. Crito presented Socrates with an opportunity to escape.

Instead of taking the easy way out by escaping his punishment, Socrates chose to stay. He would accept death before dishonor.

From Socrates, I learned a great deal. The book described his mindset, and I learned from the brilliant questions he asked, known as "Socratic questioning."

After reading several stories about his life, I stretched out on the concrete slab in one of Pierce County's jail cells. As I stared at the ceiling, I contemplated the many bad decisions of my youth, trying to connect their relationship to my predicament:

» I chose friends poorly,
» I lived a fast lifestyle, and
» I lacked discipline.

Those bad decisions led to my selling cocaine, and that crime led me to face a potential life sentence.

Even though my conviction carried the possibility of a life without parole, I believed I would return to society at some point. I began questioning whether I could do anything while serving my sentence to prepare for a better life when my prison term ended.

From Socrates, I learned the secret to success. Instead of complaining about the troubles my past decisions created, I needed to question the relationship I wanted with the broader society.

Later, I learned from many other masterminds. They taught me the timeless value of asking the right questions. For example, a well-known sales coach and motivational speaker, Zig Zigler, is famous for having said:

» "If I help other people get what they want, I can get everything that I want."

Reading about Socrates taught me to ask questions that would help me understand the people I wanted in my life. I hated confinement and didn't want to be a prisoner forever. Although I couldn't undo my past bad decisions, I started thinking about the people I wanted to interact with in the future.

Ironically, although I faced a life sentence, I didn't want to think of myself as a criminal. In the future, I wanted others to judge me for how I responded to my problems—not for the bad decisions that resulted in my imprisonment.

SOCRATIC QUESTIONING AND AVATARS:
» Who were the people I would want to interact with in the future?
» What did they do for a living?
» What influence would they have in my life?

Those kinds of questions led me to "humanize" my avatars.

WHAT'S AN AVATAR?

From my perspective, avatars were the type of people I wanted to meet in the future. They would influence aspects of my life. Although they didn't exist as flesh-and-blood people, in my mind, the avatars were lifelike—even though I didn't know who they would be.

1. I thought about my future probation officer because that person would influence my life whenever my prison term ended.
2. I thought about my prospective employer.
3. I thought about future lenders.
4. I thought about the woman I would marry and the friends I would choose.
5. Who were those people?
6. What characterized their lives?
7. What level of education would they have?
8. What could I do to earn their respect?

The more I contemplated my avatars, the more insight I had as I considered how I would adjust through my prison journey. I began with questions about whether there would be anything I could do to influence how those avatars would perceive me in the future.

The initial answer to my question was a resounding yes.

If I acted appropriately, I believed I could influence my avatars' perceptions.

As Socrates taught, one question always leads to another:

» How could I influence the perceptions of those avatars?
» What would they expect from me?

Those questions led to a three-part plan:

1. My avatars would expect me to educate myself.
2. My avatars would expect me to contribute to society.
3. My avatars would expect me to build a support network.

If I kept the expectations of my avatars at the forefront of my mind, and if I turned to those thoughts with every decision, I believed that I would influence perceptions. Instead of judging me for my criminal conviction, being a prisoner, or an ex-convict, my avatars would respect me. They would perceive me as a man of discipline and integrity, someone who worked to earn his freedom.

SELF-DIRECTED QUESTIONS:

In the pages to follow, to complete a self-directed exercise, write your responses to the following three questions.

1. If you could influence someone, who would you want to influence?
2. What do you know about that person?
3. In what ways would influencing that person change your life?
4. What steps could you take today to influence that person?

3. Sentenced to 45-Years

CHANGING THE WAY WE THINK

When justice-impacted people develop three-part plans to prepare for success after prison, they take a meaningful path that will restore confidence in times of struggle.

Federal prosecutors brought a charge known as the kingpin statute against me, Title 21 Section 848, also known as the Continuing Criminal Enterprise. When my lawyer described the charge, I didn't understand. To convict, the prosecutors would need to prove that my crime involved:

1. Three or more overt acts,
2. My supervision of five or more people, and
3. Substantial amounts of money.

Without a doubt, I knew my guilt. Yet rather than accepting responsibility and expressing remorse, I continued to live in denial—believing that I could deceive the jurors and the judge.

Despite the many people that would testify against me, I deluded myself. The jurors heard people testify. They heard from people who said that, at my direction, they rented cars to further the conspiracy, or they purchased airline tickets or rented apartments to transport and store cocaine.

The government may not have had tangible evidence that jurors could hold, but they brought forth many people who told a compelling story under oath. When the judge asked for a verdict, the jurors agreed that prosecutors had proven the case beyond a reasonable doubt. They convicted me on every count.

The statute carried a 10-year mandatory-minimum sentence, with a maximum life sentence. During that awkward transition between the time a jury convicted me and the sentencing date, a correctional officer passed me the philosophy book that told the story of Socrates, which transformed my thoughts.

if we change the way we think, we change our life.

After reading the story of Socrates, I realized I had to change. His story inspired me to stop dwelling on my past. I could use time in prison to become a better person who would be both resilient and realistic.

Socrates prompted me to lay out that three-part plan to guide my adjustment. While waiting for sentencing, I began writing extensively on how I would use time in prison to:

1. Educate myself, as evidenced by a university degree,
2. Contribute to society, as evidenced by publishing, and
3. Build a strong support network, as evidenced by mentors I would bring into my life.

To counter my commitment to change, during the sentencing hearing, the prosecutor gave his perspective:

"If Michael Santos spends every day of his life working to make amends, and if he lives to be 300 years old, our society would still be at a net loss."

The prosecutor recommended that the judge sentence me to serve a 45-year sentence, and the judge agreed.

The sentencing laws for convictions before November 1, 1987, were different. They incentivized people to use time in prison wisely. I could earn 19 years of good-time credits with my statute and sentence.

For readers who don't understand the concept of "statutory good time," it's an incentive that rewards people for avoiding disciplinary infractions while incarcerated. A person didn't need to do anything outstanding to earn good time. He simply needed to avoid being convicted of violating disciplinary infractions.

So long as I didn't lose any good time during my journey through prison, I would satisfy my sentence after 26 years. Since I was 23 when authorities took me into custody, I didn't quite know how to process the concept of serving 26 years.

Thankfully, by reading Socrates, I had a vision and a strategy. By thinking about my avatars, I could engineer a plan to advance the possibilities of emerging successfully. I would focus on that three-pronged goal:

1. Educating myself,
2. Contributing to society, and
3. Building a support network.

I began serving my sentence in the United States Penitentiary in Atlanta. The prison was thousands of miles away from where I grew up, in Seattle. While locked inside those high walls, I embarked upon the first prong of my plan.

Although I'd been a lousy student in high school, I committed to becoming a good student in prison.

Why?

Because I believed that if I could earn a university degree while incarcerated, people in society would respect me. Then I could connect the dots. If more people respected me, I believed that more opportunities would open.

Since I didn't have any financial resources, I began writing letters to universities. I wrote to hundreds of universities, not knowing whether anyone would read the letters. Still, I knew that if I didn't write letters, I wouldn't stand a chance of connecting with my avatars who lived on the other side of the walls. Each letter expressed some version of the same message:

I made terrible decisions as a young man. Because of those decisions, a judge sentenced me to serve a lengthy term in prison. I wrote that I wanted to educate myself while inside and asked for help.

In time, I found universities to work with me. I built my support network inside prison walls from the relationships I opened. The efforts resulted in earning an undergraduate degree in 1992 and a master's degree in 1995.

After Hofstra University awarded my master's degree, I began studying toward a Ph.D. at the University of Connecticut. Then a warden determined that my education had gone far enough. He stopped my formal studies by prohibiting the prison's mailroom from accepting books that the University of Connecticut's library would send for my coursework.

Fortunately, by then I had eight years of imprisonment behind me. That experience conditioned me to cope well with obstacles. While incarcerated, we must expect obstacles but work to succeed anyway.

When my formal studies came to an end, I shifted focus. As I wrote in *Earning Freedom* and other books, I went through a phase where the stock market consumed all my time. By studying how investors valued stocks, I learned about business. I became fluent in "technical analysis," understanding how to assess a stock's value in accordance with various trading patterns. Reading financial newspapers, magazines, and books, I also learned about "fundamental analysis." Those lessons taught me the importance of more objective metrics, including growth rates, profit margins, return on equity, and other factors.

Studying the stock market, I knew, would be a poor substitute for real business experience. But my long term in prison required that I look for "unorthodox" ways to prepare myself for success upon release. The more I could learn about business, the more I would arm myself for the challenges I anticipated upon release.

» What lessons could you learn with the resources you have around you?

In the following pages and chapters, you'll see how Socrates inspired me to ask those kinds of open-ended questions. The questions would not have a right answer or a wrong answer. Instead, they would prompt us to think and to continue questioning rather than complaining. I learned how to assess the opportunity costs that accompanied every decision.

Those questions helped me to accept that regardless of external factors, such as institutional rules, I could find ways to prepare for the success I wanted to build upon release. Even if the prison didn't offer classes, I could choose what I would read or what I could study. I could learn as much as possible. We could build confidence by using existing resources to prepare for a prosperous future.

Without a deliberate plan, however, we may not see the resources. Instead, we may succumb to the guidance from other people serving time around us. They may try to influence the decisions we make inside. Their advice could lead us to a different outcome from what we want.

In the following pages, I'll reveal more about the strategy that worked so well for me. I'll recommend readers compare that strategy with other adjustment patterns.

As we approached the turn of the century, I crossed into the second half of my sentence. I had 13 years behind me and 13 years of prison ahead of me. I shifted my attention to writing, wanting to advance toward the other two prongs of my adjustment strategy. First, I wrote articles and submitted them for publication. Then I began writing chapters for academic books.

In time, one of my mentors offered to introduce me to his publisher. Professor George Cole, from the University of Connecticut, presided over my Ph.D. program, and he authored the leading textbook on corrections. George suggested I write a book for an academic audience that his publisher could package as a supplemental text for university students in criminal justice courses. His suggestion led to my first book, *About Prison*.

In retrospect, it's easy to connect the dots. In earlier chapters, I wrote about how I contemplated my avatars. To recap:

1. While still in the county jail, before a judge sentenced me, I thought about the people I would want to influence in my future.
2. I didn't know George Cole then, and George Cole didn't know me. He was a distinguished author, and he led the criminal justice department at the University of Connecticut.
3. While locked in the Pierce County Jail, masterminds like Socrates inspired me. They taught me to ask "Socratic questions" about what steps I could take during my imprisonment to prepare for success. Those questions led to my three-part adjustment strategy:
4. My avatars would expect me to educate myself.
5. My avatars would expect me to contribute to society.
6. My avatars would expect me to build a support network.
7.
8. By sticking to that three-pronged strategy, I could open more opportunities.
9. Since I executed that plan, I earned university degrees.
10. Since I earned university degrees, I found it easier to open opportunities to publish articles.
11. Since I published articles, I found mentors like George Cole.

12. George didn't judge me for the bad decisions that brought me to prison. Instead, he looked upon me as someone who could add value to society. George then introduced me to his publisher. She issued a contract to publish *About Prison*. Thousands of people became aware of my work when *About Prison* came out. My support network grew.

13. Since the prison system didn't allow me to "run a business," I assigned royalties from *About Prison* to family members. Those resources opened opportunities I could leverage and create more opportunities.

The cycle of success began when I served time in jail—before a judge sentenced me to prison.

I urge readers to respond to the following question:

» When will your cycle of success begin?

I'm convinced it will begin as soon as you start living by the same model that leaders taught me:

1. Visualize success by contemplating avatars,
2. Create a plan to persuade avatars to invest time, energy, and resources in your development.
3. Execute your plan with every thought, word, and decision you make while serving your sentence.

After writing my first book, I reached out to another mentor. Dr. Marilyn McShane. Marilyn taught criminal justice courses at several universities. She also advised publishing companies and opened an opportunity to publish my second book, *Profiles from Prison*, through Greenwood/Praeger, another well-respected academic publishing house.

With two publishing credentials behind me, I aspired to reach a wider audience. Prison populations had been growing, and I thought writing a general nonfiction book about the prison system would be helpful. I pulled books from prison library shelves and researched how to go about publishing a mainstream book.

1. The first step would be to write a book proposal.
2. Then I would need to write sample chapters.

3. Next, I would need to write a cover letter and begin sending self-ad-dressed-stamped envelopes to literary agents.

Research showed that if I could persuade a literary agent to represent me, the literary agent would connect with publishing houses. If editors who worked at the publishing house liked my book, the editor would issue a contract to bring my book to market. It wouldn't be easy.

Fortunately, living in prison had conditioned me to deal with rejection.

The book proposal required about 30 pages of writing. Sample chapters added another 30 pages. Postage and copy costs would be too high if I were to send the entire package to scores of publishers. I needed to create more economical tactics.

Instead of sending the complete book-proposal package, I leveraged my earlier work.

First, I identified 100 literary agents. Then I wrote a query letter describing my background, educational credentials, publishing credentials, and a few sentences about the type of book I wanted to write. I sent that one-page letter and a self-addressed stamped envelope to the agents. With postage costs and copying, the total cash outlay amounted to less than $2 an envelope—or $200.

» What value would you place on that $200 investment?

Each person would have to ask such questions. This question helps us appreciate the meaning of the phrase: "The right decision at the wrong time is the wrong decision."

1. Had I not spent the early years of my sentence working to develop writing and communication skills, I would not have persuaded leaders like George Cole to mentor me.
2. Without mentors like George Cole, publishers would not have brought my earlier books to market.
3. If I didn't have earlier publishing credentials, a literary agent would not have interest in working with me.

As an orderly in prison, my wages amounted to about $10 per month. The $200 I spent on postage represented more than a year's worth of income from my job. Yet by sending out those letters, I secured a relationship with a literary agent.

I sent the agent my full proposal. The literary agent secured a publishing contract with St. Martin's Press within two weeks. The contract came with compensation that brought over 1,000 times the initial investment I made in postage. More importantly, libraries and bookstores across the country began selling the book I wrote for a general, nonfiction audience.

St. Martin's Press published *Inside: Life Behind Bars in America* in 2006. The investment of time and energy continues to bear fruit and pay dividends. Twice a year, I receive a royalty check from the publishing house.

Many opportunities opened through the books I wrote. The books persuaded people to believe that I didn't just "talk" about wanting to live a life of meaning, relevance, and contribution. Those people had tangible proof. They wanted to invest in me, help me, and believe in me.

Any person in prison can begin creating credentials that will advance prospects for success. It's never too early and never too late to start preparing for a life of meaning, relevance, and dignity.

My adjustment plan had three components that aligned with how I defined success:
1. My avatars would expect me to educate myself.
2. They would expect me to contribute to society.
3. They would expect me to build a support network.

SELF-DIRECTED QUESTIONS:

In the pages to follow, to complete a self-directed exercise, write your responses to the following three questions.

1. How would each of those components work together?
2. What opportunities open for people who strive to contribute to society?
3. How would your efforts to contribute to your community influence leaders to mentor you?

4. Carole

BUILDING A LOVING RELATIONSHIP FROM PRISON

To succeed after prison, start by engineering a plan that will bring more people into your life. Give them the reasons to invest in you and your dreams.

Our decisions in prison influence the opportunities that open for us.

When I began serving my sentence, many people offered their thoughts on how to serve a sentence. They suggested that the best way to fill time would be to forget about the world outside and focus on time inside.

If a person chooses to focus on time inside, the person must also accept the consequences. He may not like the result. As the person focuses on fitting in with the prison expectations, he may find fewer opportunities to succeed when he gets out. Statistics show that the more time we spend in corrections, the more likely we struggle with underemployment, unemployment, or even homelessness. Those problems can lead to further problems with the law and a return trip to prison.

Instead of distancing myself from society, I chose to build bridges and connect. That strategy broadened my support network. It led to correspondence with Carole, a friendship, and then to our wedding inside a federal prison's visiting room on June 24, 2003, as I completed my 16th year. We'd have to spend ten years apart before we could live together.

Carole became my liaison to the world. I'd write by hand and send my manuscripts to her. She'd interact with publishers or work to bring my projects to life. If I hadn't sown seeds early in my journey, Carole would never have begun a romantic relationship with me. She didn't only become the love of my life, but she also provided further evidence that if we pursue a deliberate strategy, we can transcend the challenges of confinement:

1. Start by defining success as the best possible outcome,
2. Create a plan,
3. Set priorities that will advance the plan in incremental steps,
4. Develop tools, tactics, and resources that promote each phase of the plan, and
5. Execute the plan every day.

Together, Carole and I worked to create a quasi-business, despite our unconventional life.

1. My writing generated revenues that supported my wife.
2. We paid taxes.
3. Revenues from my writing projects allowed Carole to work toward a nursing degree.

All our efforts would relate to a strategic plan. The plan would allow Carole to live a sustainable life while I prepared for a meaningful career upon release. She relocated to live in the community where I served my sentence. When authorities transferred me to another prison, Carole would relocate with me. We visited every day that the rules would authorize.

Besides writing books under my name, I began ghostwriting books for other people to advance our projects. Every decision I made in prison began with one question:

» Will this decision lead to success upon release?

That strategy empowered me through the journey.
1. It dictated the books that I read while I served the sentence.
2. It dictated the people with whom I associated.
3. It dictated the jobs I tried to secure in prison.
4. It dictated my efforts to persuade counselors to assign me to a bunk that would minimize exposure to volatility.

In later chapters, readers will see how that strategy influenced higher income opportunities upon release and higher levels of liberty. Higher levels of income and

freedom created new opportunities. They allowed me to build an asset portfolio that would contribute to my financial security.

The adjustment in prison led to more than $1 million in appreciating assets and more than $500,000 in equity within 28 months of release. People striving for a better life after prison may modify this strategy to suit their definition of success. They can begin by asking Socratic questions throughout the journey and projecting how today's decisions will influence their desired results.

More than anything, I wanted to emerge successfully. Daily decisions related to what I wanted to achieve in months, years, and decades ahead. When reading a book, for example, I'd read with a purpose. When I finished reading the book, I'd write a report in accordance with the following format:

1. Date I read the book:
2. Why did I choose to read this book?
3. What did I learn from reading this book?
4. How will this book contribute to my prospects for success upon release?

Adhering to that strategy made me more selective with what I read. Reading takes time, and I wanted to get the most value from the time I invested in personal development. Then, I worked to harness the value and create an asset—the book report. Later, I anticipated I could use the book report as validation, showing others how I used time in prison to prepare for success. Every decision directly connected to the success I felt determined to become.

Many opportunity costs and risks accompany our decisions. Since I knew that many people in prison placed a high value on where they positioned their seats in a television viewing area or whether they had the authority to change a channel, I avoided television rooms.

Every decision began with a question that related to the life I wanted to lead when authorities released me:

1. If I choose to watch television, will that decision advance or hinder my prospects for success upon release?
2. If I play organized sports, will that decision advance or hinder my chances for success upon release?

3. If I play table games, will that decision advance or hinder my prospects for success upon release?
4. If I associate with one person or another, will that decision promote or hinder my opportunities for success upon release?
5. If I participate in this program, will that decision advance or hinder my prospects for success upon release?
6. If I express my opinion around others, will that decision advance or hinder my prospects for success upon release?

Each question had a purpose.

Rather than making decisions that would ease my journey, enhance my reputation in prison, or advance my standing with other people, I considered the avatars. I didn't know the avatars, but each of them existed in my mind, and they felt lifelike.

I considered the people with whom I wanted to associate in the future. Then I contemplated whether my decisions would show good judgment. How would my decision influence the possibility of support from the avatars I wanted in my life?

If my decisions followed that "principled" pathway, I built confidence. I didn't feel the pain of multiple decades in prison when I empowered myself. Instead, each decision represented a new investment in personal development that would lead to higher levels of success.

I wasn't perfect, of course. I made some bad decisions along the way. Yet, adhering to the strategy always helped me get back on track.

» In what ways could this strategy help you?

FINAL PREPARATIONS BEFORE RELEASE FROM PRISON:

As I advanced through my final years of imprisonment, I could reflect on the totality of my journey. Leaders taught me lessons that helped my adjustment. I felt a duty and responsibility to pass those lessons along. When I got out, I wanted to continue following those lessons, but I also wanted to impact the lives of millions of others. In my view, mass incarceration represented one of the great social injustices

of our time. Improving outcomes for people who went through the system felt like a goal worth pursuing.

But I also would need to earn a living. To build a career around my journey, I needed to create products that would communicate a message. Specifically, I wanted to document the journey. Others would like resources to sustain energy and discipline over a long period. They would also need guidance on how to stay focused in the short term.

I began creating resources that I could use to teach others.

Some readers may be familiar with self-help literature. From my perspective, self-help literature reveals a similar recipe. People succeed when they follow a pattern that others have used to achieve high levels of success.

1. Socrates began revealing that pattern more than 2,500 years ago.
2. The Bible told those same stories more than 2,000 years ago.

Since the invention of the printing press, we've used printed words to convey ideas. Those ideas reveal patterns that anyone can follow.

The journey of life always includes struggle. A person will struggle through life, whether in prison or in society. We can always find strategies to make it through if we read about others. Authors have written about that pathway in self-help literature since the beginning of the printed word.

We read that message through the writings of Socrates, Mahatma Gandhi, Viktor Frankl, Nelson Mandela, and Aleksander Solzhenitsyn. We read the same message from people who studied struggle and figured out ways to overcome it. Work that makes this truism self-evident includes the writing of Stephen Covey, Joel Osteen, and Anthony Robbins. We see the same message in the careers and contributions of Jack Welch, Bill Gates, and Steve Jobs.

WHAT IS A COHERENT MESSAGE?

1. Leaders begin by clearly defining success.
2. They contemplate the pain or challenge they're experiencing at a given time.
3. They consider steps to a better outcome.

4. They create a plan that will lead them to success.
5. They understand how to set priorities.
6. Then they execute the plan.

Individuals who aspire to succeed always follow that pattern. Those who reach their highest potential follow the pattern in sports, business, politics, marriage, and in any area of life where they want to excel. They always know where they are and where they're going. They create plans and strategies, and make decisions in accordance with those plans and strategies.

To build a career around my journey, I needed to craft products and services that would communicate that message. With that end in mind, I began writing specific books.

I wrote *Earning Freedom: Conquering a 45-Year Prison Term* to show people how to build strength while crossing through years or decades of struggle. *Earning Freedom* provides many details I left out in this synopsis. It begins with the day of my arrest, on August 11, 1987, until the day that I transitioned to a halfway house, on August 13, 2012.

I wrote *Prison! My 8,344th Day* because I wanted readers to see what it meant to make disciplined decisions daily, regardless of external factors. The book provides a glimpse of a typical day during my 23rd year of confinement. I begin the book by writing about my eyes opening in the morning. The book concludes when I lie down on my rack to sleep. It covers a single day, describing what it means to make disciplined, deliberate decisions while living amidst persistent challenges.

Then I wrote two separate books to describe the deliberate strategy I teach. I wrote *Triumph! The Straight-A Guide* for adults in the criminal justice system, and I wrote *Success! The Straight-A Guide for At-Risk Youth* for juveniles. Each book conveys the same message, but I wrote them for specific audiences.

In writing those books, I intended to build products I could use to advance my career upon release.

Since the day Carole married me in a federal prison's visiting room, authorities transferred me to the following institutions:

» Florence, Colorado

» Lompoc, California
» Taft, California, and
» Atwater, California

With each transfer, Carole packed up and moved so we could spend as much time visiting as possible. Together, we made plans for the life we would build when I got out. She became a certified nurse's aide. Then, after working through the pre-requisites of nursing school, she earned credentials to work as a licensed vocational nurse, then in 2010, she became a registered nurse.

We chose nursing for her career because nursing would allow her to earn a livable wage regardless of where authorities sent me. Further, by acquiring a license to practice as a registered nurse, we anticipated that Carole would earn a sufficient income to support our family after my release. Her earnings would allow me to work toward building my career—a career that I anticipated would take several years to develop.

While I worked to create a regular income stream or multiple income streams, Carole's earnings as a nurse would bring stability to our family.

Readers with time to serve in prison should anticipate income streams upon release.

1. Where will your income originate?
2. How much will you earn?
3. How will those earnings advance your stability?

By using the Socratic questioning approach, Carole and I could make plans to advance our success prospects.

Since I served longer than a quarter century, I didn't have roots anywhere. As we approached the end of my term, we had to figure out where we wanted to live. We chose California because I considered the state a big market that offered the best opportunities for me, given the support network I'd built. Besides the possibilities, I liked the weather.

Toward the end of my sentence, while confined in a camp near Bakersfield, California, I met Justin Paperny. Justin had built a career as a stockbroker before getting into trouble with the law. He served a relatively brief sentence for violating securities laws.

We became friends. Justin's conviction meant he needed to create a new career upon release. In 2008, the nation's economy deteriorated, sinking into the most significant recession of our time.

I used Socratic questioning to help Justin see the challenges that awaited him.

1. "How do you plan on earning a living when you get out?"
2. "How will the market respond to your conviction?"
3. "Why would a manager hire you when so many people without felony convictions are looking for employment?"
4. "In what ways could you turn your experience of going through the criminal justice system into a strength?"

Those questions stumped Justin. He didn't know how to answer because he limited his thoughts to why prosecutors and a judge put him in prison.

With questions, he could see the societal problems. We could work together to build solutions.

Millions of formerly incarcerated individuals would face the same challenges that would complicate Justin's life once he got out. Prison isn't the only problem. We saw a massive problem with all that transpired after prison. People would need to transition into the job market.

I suggested that Justin join efforts I'd been making to create programs and services that improve outcomes for the formerly incarcerated. We launched a plan that would leverage our strengths. Although I would have to serve three more years in prison, I could use my time to write programs, lessons, books, and courses. Since Justin would be free, he could leverage the resources I created, using them to achieve our objective of improving outcomes for justice-impacted people at every stage of the journey.

When Justin completed his prison term, he established a nonprofit. With an authorized nonprofit, I could begin writing proposals for grants to fund our work. Those efforts led to us receiving funding from philanthropic foundations. They pro-

vided resources to grow. Through our work, we could build solutions to improve outcomes for people in our nation's criminal justice system.

Had I not learned to ask the right questions early during my prison journey, I would not have been able to plan. Without a plan, I wouldn't have a personal-development guide. The project helped me to set priorities. First, I worked to educate myself and build credentials. If I hadn't earned credentials, I wouldn't have been able to persuade publishers to bring my books to market. If I hadn't brought books to market, I wouldn't have persuaded foundations to provide financial resources.

I'd need to continue that same strategy upon release.

Setting clear goals characterized my entire journey in prison, and the strategy still guides me today. When I reached the end of my sentence, I knew what I would need to ease my transition into society. At a minimum, I wanted:

1. Sufficient savings to sustain me for the first year in society.
2. Income opportunities waiting.
3. A clear plan to guide me through the first year in liberty.

I'm hopeful that readers in custody will see the relationship between decisions and success. I believe those who make conscientious, values-based, goal-oriented choices have a greater chance of success than those who simply allow the calendar pages to turn.

The skills I developed during the first decade of imprisonment led to opportunities in subsequent decades. They helped me create opportunities to add value in society. I could also add value for other people in prison, helping them write their books.

Although prison rules prevented me from "running a business," by understanding how the system operated, I could find ways to balance. Every decision contributed to a systematic plan to ease my transition upon release. Executing that strategy every day allowed me to return to society strong.

Carole and I had more than $85,000 in the bank on the day of my release. More importantly, we had a plan to guide our future.

I did not originate the strategy to succeed upon release. Lessons from leaders empowered me through the journey. Those same lessons can empower others. In writing books, I shared what I learned from the world's leaders. Even in the context of a prison experience, those lessons advance prospects for success. Through those books, I documented the result of making values-based, goal-oriented decisions.

The remainder of this book will describe how other people in prison can do the same.

Regardless of where you are today, what decisions you've made in the past, and what conditions you're living in, you have the power to begin sowing seeds for a brighter future.

Remember that every decision comes with opportunity costs. To the extent that you adhere to a disciplined, deliberate, strategic path, you can build a life of significance, relevance, and meaning.

SELF-DIRECTED QUESTIONS:

In the pages to follow, to complete a self-directed exercise, write your responses to the following three questions.

1. Who are your avatars, and how do they relate to the success you want to build?
2. What would they expect of you?
3. In what ways are the decisions you're making today leading you closer to earning support tomorrow?

5. Halfway House
BUILDING TOOLS, TACTICS, AND RESOURCES

After 25 years in prison, I transfer to a halfway house to serve my final year with the Bureau of Prisons. The decisions at the start of the sentence influenced the liberty I had at the end.

People assigned to the dorm of the Atwater camp were still sleeping when I woke on August 12, 2012. Over the past several years, I adjusted my daily routine to wake when others slept and to sleep while others ran around the housing unit. I used earplugs to block the noise and a mask to cover my eyes. By 3:00 a.m., I pushed myself through my last exercise session from inside a federal prison, wondering how my life would change after I walked out.

I had 9,135 days of imprisonment behind me, just over 25 years. At 9:00 a.m., Carole would drive to the prison, and together we'd drive to the halfway house in the Tenderloin District of downtown San Francisco. My case manager recommended me for the maximum placement I could receive in a Residential Reentry Center. I appreciated the privilege of serving the final 365 days of my sentence in the halfway house.

After my exercise, I walked around the track alone, reflecting on the entire journey and all I learned. I went to the chapel and prayed for guidance. I knew the world had changed in many ways since I started serving my sentence, but I felt ready.

In truth, I felt as prepared as I ever would have been after I served eight years in prison. By then, I had a master's degree and knew I would never violate a law again. Since mechanisms didn't exist to advance my release date, I would have to climb through 16 more years. As I sat in that chapel waiting, I thanked God for protecting me through the journey and for my many blessings, especially Carole.

Finally, an announcement over the loudspeaker instructed me to report to the rear gate.

I walked through gates that separated the minimum-security camp from the penitentiary. Officers escorted me to the discharge area and began to process me. A staff member handed me a few hundred dollars in cash from my account and indicated that I'd receive a check for the remainder.

That was it. I walked outside and met Carole. She wore a yellow dress with a yellow ribbon tied around her waist. With tears of joy in her eyes, she hugged me, and we drove off to start our journey together.

Although we were together for the first time, we weren't free. The case manager told me that I would have to report to the San Francisco Halfway House within three hours of my release. Carole showed me a map indicating that the drive would take three hours, so we didn't have time for diversions.

We wanted to be together, of course. The time crunch, however, dictated that we needed to get on the road. I had heard from others that if I didn't get to the halfway house in time, the case manager would deny my request for home visits for several weeks. To avoid that complication, we resisted the urge to stop for alone time, and we drove straight to the halfway house.

Once we got into the car and buckled in, Carole passed me an iPhone. Smartphones didn't exist when I started my sentence. I'd seen phones on television, but I had never held one. I put the phone to my ear. Since I didn't hear a dial tone, I thought the phone didn't work, even though I saw the lighted face with all the apps. She laughed as she showed me how to use it. Before that day, I'd never sent an email, watched a YouTube video, or accessed the internet.

Technology fascinated me, even though I didn't know how to use it.

While in prison, I frequently dreamed about the internet, wondering how to use it as a tool or how it would contribute to my career. I read many books and articles to learn about the power of the web and even leveraged my relationships to participate indirectly.

Since the late 1990s, I have had a web presence. I persuaded people in my support network to build websites for me. They published my articles, and they'd send images that showed how my website looked to visitors of MichaelSantos.com.

But there wasn't any real way to experience the web without computer access. Reading about the internet seemed about as authentic as reading about playing tennis. But without getting online, I didn't know how to appreciate the power of technology fully. When Carole gave me an iPhone, I got my first chance. As she drove, I played around with the phone, calling family and friends.

Carole and I spoke about our plans. Goals carried me through the 25 years inside, and I pledged to continue living a values-based, goal-oriented life. During my final year in the halfway house, I vowed to sow seeds that would allow us to start my career. I intended to:

1. Create products and services that would improve outcomes for people in the criminal justice system.
2. Create a business model to help more formerly incarcerated people transition into the job market.
3. Create campaigns that would spread awareness of why reforming our criminal justice system made sense. I wanted to think innovatively in ways that would inspire more people to pursue paths that would lead to success upon release.
4. Create multiple revenue streams that would build stability for Carole and me.

But first things first. During my year in the halfway house, I needed to establish myself.

Fortunately, I had begun making plans long before I left prison. I had job opportunities waiting. I had money in the bank. I had an extensive support network. Further, I had a product line to launch with the different books I wrote while serving my sentence. My books included:

1. Inside: Life Behind Bars in America
2. Earning Freedom: Conquering a 45-Year Prison Term
3. Prison! My 8,344th Day
4. Triumph! The Straight-A Guide For Conquering Imprisonment and Preparing for Reentry
5. Success! The Straight-A Guide for At-Risk Youth
6. Profiles from Prison
7. About Prison

I wouldn't describe the books I wrote as masterpieces of English literature. Instead, they served a purpose: to help people understand prisons, the people they hold, and strategies for growing through challenges successfully.

I hoped my books would lead to credibility as I ventured into the world to start my career. I intended to use the books as tools, resources I could leverage to build a business or income streams.

My friend and business partner, Justin, also provided a lot of help. Justin had built a consulting business, using the lessons I wrote when we were together. People going into the system could use those lessons to get a better outcome, and Justin provided one-on-one consulting services. I created a head start by working with Justin to launch that business while we served our sentences. Because of those efforts, income opportunities for ghostwriting books opened within days of getting out.

Experienced convinced me that anyone could use deliberate strategies to reject negativity or overcome challenges. That universal message applies to anyone and everyone. If deliberate strategies could empower me through decades, others could also use them to achieve more.

People going into the system, or those serving time, should contemplate steps they can begin taking now. Regardless of external circumstances, I learned that options always existed. Regardless of what rules govern our lives at present, we can work to build skills that will influence the people we're going to meet and the opportunities that will open for us. We may not be able to change our current predicament, but we can always work to change ourselves.

HALFWAY TO LIBERTY

I'll never forget my thoughts as Carole drove me across the Bay Bridge, taking us from Richmond to San Francisco. The majestic skyline inspired me. I felt so good to be in a major American city.

Carole dropped me off in front of the halfway house, and the staff buzzed me inside. I didn't have any trouble navigating the rules. After decades inside, everything seemed easy. The intake officer assigned me to a two-person room, but my roommate wasn't there. I sat in a chair and began experimenting with the iPhone, connecting with the world.

Although I got to the halfway house on a Monday, my case manager, Charles, didn't meet with me until Thursday. While doing his intake paperwork, Charles commented on the length of time that I'd served. He suggested that I participate in counseling sessions to help me acclimate.

Before going to that meeting, I prepared for such a recommendation by gathering:

» Books I wrote,
» Support letters I'd received,
» Curriculum vitae that listed my published writings, and
» Job offer from an employer confirming that I could start working as soon as the halfway house authorized me to begin.

"How did you get all this done while you were in prison?" He did not expect to see so many resources from someone who served 25 years.

As Charles flipped through the books, I could sense how the tangible work I presented influenced his perception. Instead of seeing me as the ex-convict who served a quarter century and needed counseling, he treated me as a man. The case manager said he would give me as much liberty as his position authorized. When he excused me from having to waste time in the counseling classes, I felt relieved. In an instant, I had credibility with him, and to the extent he was able, Charles agreed to assist with the plan I laid out for my first year in society.

That initial meeting with Charles went well. Without a doubt, I felt fortunate to have him as my case manager, as I know it could have gone differently. Had I not brought those tangible resources with me, I would have had to waste hours going through several classes before I would qualify for work release. He treated me with dignity as if we were two men rather than as if I were an inferior human being just released from prison.

Why?

The roots for that successful meeting extended way back to the 1980s when I waited for sentencing from inside the special housing unit of the Pierce County Jail.

Recap?

While in my cell, I read about Socrates. From his story, I learned the importance of living for something greater than myself. Instead of dwelling on the challenges of my decisions, I could empower myself by thinking about others. Through Socratic questioning, I could learn the relationship between my decisions and how others would perceive me.

With that insight, I began contemplating people like Charles—case managers and probation officers—before my judge even imposed my 45-year sentence. They were my avatars. I could create plans to influence their perceptions by thinking about what they would expect.

I believed I could influence a better outcome upon release by executing those plans every day of my sentence. Those plans gave me hope and helped me to restore confidence—as if I could control some aspect of my life.

Still, I felt fortunate to have a case manager who treated me well.

Some readers may be familiar with the social scientist Abraham Maslow and his theory about the hierarchy of needs. Maslow wrote that we could not reach our highest potential unless we first satisfied our basic needs. For example, to appreciate the value of education or art, we first need to make sure we have basic needs like food, clothing, and shelter. The same principle would apply to my adjustment in society.

I needed identification to make a complete adjustment after a quarter century of confinement. For the past month, I'd been studying a handbook from the Department of Motor Vehicles, and I asked Charles for permission to go to the Department of Motor Vehicles. I wanted to register for the driving test.

He granted my first pass for three hours, allowing me to walk to the DMV.

SELF-DIRECTED QUESTIONS:

In the pages to follow, to complete a self-directed exercise, write your responses to the following three questions.

1. What strategy have you put in place to influence your transition from prison to society?
2. What will your case manager think about you the day you transition to a halfway house?
3. What can you begin doing today to influence the level of liberty your case manager will grant?

6. First Community Pass

SOWING EARLY SEEDS FOR SUCCESS

After 25 years in prison, I began to explore the streets of San Francisco with my first community pass from the halfway house at 111 Taylor Street.

On August 13, 2012, a few days after walking out, I headed to the Department of Motor Vehicles. Spending that time in the car with Carole felt great, as it was the first time I'd been out of prison boundaries since 1987. Yet since we only had a short window before the halfway house expected me, I didn't fully appreciate the liberty. The pressure of getting to my destination on time blocked me from thoroughly enjoying the experience.

With that pass to leave the halfway house, I felt different. From the moment I pushed open the door and walked onto Taylor Street, I felt amazingly free—but also directionless. I had to navigate through busy streets to the Department of Motor Vehicles on Fell Street in San Francisco. Carole had told me how to use an app on my phone that would, in theory, provide directions. But I didn't know how to use it. Instead, I called my business partner Justin. He offered the step-by-step guidance I needed to reach my destination.

I looked forward to getting my driver's license, an essential resource for developing my career. Before getting out, my wife sent me a handbook so I could study for the written portion of the test. I studied it thoroughly and felt confident that I could pass. When it came to the driving part of the test, I wasn't so sure.

People think that a person who knows how to drive never forgets. Such people did not serve multiple decades in prison. While Carole drove me from the prison to the halfway house, I sensed that I no longer knew how to drive. The cars zipped by in the other lane, making me dizzy as I watched.

While incarcerated, our bodies don't move any faster than our legs can carry us, and our eyes adjust to the slower pace. Once we get out, we must adapt to the fast pace of the real world. Although I looked forward to taking the written exam, I'd have to practice before scheduling the driving portion of the exam.

After finishing the written exam, I walked back to the halfway house. With money in my pocket, I felt the call of Burger King. For decades, I ate in chow halls with guards watching or alone by the bunk in my cubicle or cell. I savored the thought of biting into an American cheeseburger. I dropped more than $30 in that restaurant, buying Whoppers, French fries, onion rings, milkshakes, and sodas. And I ate everything.

When I returned to the halfway house, showing that I had passed the written exam, Charles permitted me to practice driving with Carole. I didn't know I forgot how to drive or when I forgot. It may have happened after ten years, maybe after 20. When Carole and I started to practice, it became clear that I lacked confidence behind the wheel.

After a few days of driving with Carole, I felt ready for the exam, and fortunately, I passed. With a license, I felt like I'd crossed off one of the first challenges of returning to society.

FAMILY AND WORK:

Since I had job prospects waiting, Charles authorized me to shop for clothing I would need for work. Since I didn't have much time, Carole and my younger sister, Christina, met me at the Westfield Mall in San Francisco on my first weekend at the halfway house. The shopping trip became a mini-family reunion after 25 years. My sister could see how excited I felt to blend in with society, and I told her about the job opportunity.

Several years before my release, I met Lee, a great human being and an extraordinary businessman. The strategy I used to get into school or to overcome other obstacles proved helpful in many ways—including opening mentor relationships. Routinely, I'd write unsolicited letters to people that inspired me. Since Lee had built several remarkable businesses that employed hundreds of people, generating billions in revenue, I knew I could learn much from him.

Over time, Lee became one of my closest friends, mentors, and business partners. He visited me frequently during my final years. When he came, he asked how

I intended to earn a living when I got out. I explained the complexities that I had learned from interviewing others. I would need to satisfy specific conditions that included employment. In other words, I needed to show that I had a steady paycheck before authorities would authorize me to go out on my own to build my business.

Lee listened as I made a case on why I could bring value to his company if he would allow me to earn a paycheck.

Lee did more than anyone could ask. He said he would give me a desk and a paycheck when I got out. While I served my final year in the halfway house, one of Lee's businesses would pay me $10 per hour to satisfy the requirements for the halfway house.

As Lee and I sat in his office, he invited me to start training alongside him. Wanting to impact the lives of other justice-impacted people, I told him that I needed to spend those initial months learning about technology. "I'll give you a year to build a business," he said. "If you can't make something happen within a year, then come work with me, and we'll build a business together."

I am lucky to have built a friendship with a leader like Lee. A coalition of influential friends can help anyone emerge from struggle. Many wise men who lived before me have found truth in the saying:

» "The harder I work, the luckier I get."

Lee embodied all the good characteristics and traits that I aspired to develop. Over time, he proved himself as an innovative and gifted businessman. Further, he contributed to his community, providing opportunities and resources that influenced thousands of lives.

When I contemplated avatars or thought about the type of people I wanted to emulate upon release, I visualized leaders like Lee. Before making strategic decisions, I'd introspect, asking the rhetorical question:

» "What Would Lee Do?"

Leaders always leave us clues on how they became successful.

Because I had a vision of connecting with people like Lee, I had to figure out what Lee and leaders like him would expect of me. He didn't know me when I began serving my sentence. My conviction showed that I spent the 1980s as a reckless young man who sold cocaine. A judge sentenced me to serve a 45-year sentence. If I didn't do something to change perceptions, people would always see me as a criminal.

I could create new pathways by focusing on avatars and contemplating what they would expect of me. Masterminds convinced me that by working to educate myself, contributing to society, and building a support network, I could persuade influential and successful people to believe in me. This "mastermind" strategy characterized the life of every successful person I met.

Anyone serving time in prison could begin sowing seeds to develop support from leaders like Lee. Opportunities that opened for me throughout my journey were available to everyone around me. When I started serving my sentence, I didn't have any financial resources. Nor did I have an education.

Reading Socrates gave me the advantage of hope. Hope for a better future led me to seek wisdom. I found the recipe for that wisdom from masterminds, first Socrates, then many others. They taught me the art of question-based learning. By contemplating the best possible outcome and questioning what my avatars would expect, I crafted a strategy that would lead to success.

STEAL IDEAS FROM MASTERMINDS:

As Steve Jobs, another mastermind, said, "Good artists copy ideas, but great artists steal ideas." To prepare for success, I copied ideas from the most successful masterminds I could find, whether they lived thousands of years ago or whether they served time alongside me in federal prison. As I saw it, masterminds were all around us.

Regardless of our status today, we all have masterminds around us. When communicating with people in prison, I challenge them to question their actions and choices. How will those actions and choices influence masterminds? If they perceive a person as worthy of their time, they willingly help and invest. I cannot recall how many people invested time, energy, and resources in my success, even though I did not know them before my imprisonment. They saw me as being authentic, and they wanted to help.

I found that I could "will" avatars into my life who would invest in my future. And if I could do that while serving 26 years, then just think what you can do!

Some people who invested in me along the way include the following:

1. Prison staff members who allowed me to maneuver my way into the right type of job—a job that would allow me to make progress toward the independent goals I set.
2. Lawyers who came into my life and volunteered their time to advance my release date—although I served every day of my sentence, I appreciated their efforts.
3. Mentors and educators who visited me at their own expense, regardless of my location.
4. Publishers who opened a platform for me to bring books to market.
5. Other people in prison who became friends throughout the journey.
6. Investors who provided financial resources that would allow me to advance my goals.
7. Business owners who agreed to open introductions for me upon release.
8. Carole, who became my wife and life partner.

Whether I served time in jail, a high-security penitentiary, a medium-security prison, a low-security prison, or a minimum-security camp, I always found masterminds. They expressed interest and wanted to help. If this strategy only succeeded for me in a single minimum-security camp, then people could say I was lucky. My earlier books showed that many people came into my life and helped advance my prospects for success.

All people can invite the same types of support into their life.

1. First, people must begin asking the types of Socratic questions that allowed me to find mentors.
2. Then, they needed to create a plan.
3. Finally, they needed to execute the plan as the days turned into weeks, the weeks turned into months, the months turned into years, and for some, the years turned into decades.

My job with Lee's company satisfied Charles, my case manager. Since I had a place to work, he authorized me to leave the halfway house each morning at 6:00 a.m. I didn't return to the halfway house until around 8:00 in the evening. I provided

Charles with a copy of my check stub and a money order for 25% of my gross wages on payday. So long as I complied with his terms, he lived up to his word and allowed me all the liberty I needed to begin building my career.

ESTABLISHING CREDIT:

With a driver's license, a job, and a paycheck, I had to begin building a banking relationship. After I received my first paycheck, I went to Bank of America and opened an account. Since Charles had told me that I could not apply for credit until after I completed my obligation to the Bureau of Prisons, I opened a checking account and a savings account.

When the banker ran a credit report, we learned I had a 0-0-0 credit score. He asked how a person my age could proceed through life without accumulating a credit score—good or bad. The banker listened with interest as I told him I'd just concluded 25 years in custody and that I was living in a halfway house. That conversation opened another opportunity for me to tell the story of my journey, another opportunity to influence a potential source of support.

Many people emerge from prison and try to hide their past. I don't judge how much information an individual should reveal. In my case, I've found that total transparency always served me best. By being completely honest about my past, I've always found that people were willing to listen. With the record I built while inside, even bankers willingly welcomed me home and encouraged me. When rules would allow me to apply for credit, he assured me that Bank of America would be ready to help.

Over the next several weeks, many of the seeds I'd planted while incarcerated began to bear fruit. As mentioned in my other books, I wrote articles routinely while I served my sentence. The articles I wrote related to the prison system or overcoming struggles and helped me build interest or a brand. I became somewhat of a subject-matter authority. As a strategy to broaden awareness of my work, I asked my wife to hire a web developer to build a website where I could publish the articles I wrote. We had our strategy: I would write by hand and send the articles home. Carole would type the articles and publish them on my website or other media sites she maintained on my behalf.

MEDIA ATTENTION:

While in the halfway house, I received an email from Vlae Kershner, a news director at the *San Francisco Chronicle*. Vlae told me that he had been following the work I published on the web for years and asked whether I'd be interested in the newspaper writing a profile about my return to society after a quarter century. That conversation led to an interview and a front-page story in one of the most highly visible newspapers in the world. The San Francisco newspaper published the article on Thanksgiving weekend, about 100 days after I transitioned to the halfway house in 2012.

Instead of focusing on my crime or the decades I served, it profiled my efforts to improve outcomes for justice-impacted people and the system. The article brought publicity that validated my work. A person couldn't buy that type of coverage, and I intended to leverage the article in ways that would open new opportunities. With the newspaper story, people would judge me for how I responded to my lengthy sentence rather than for the bad decisions I began making at 20.

Those who choose to live transparently and authentically may also find that this strategy would advance their prospects for success. People are more receptive to extending "second chances" or opportunities to people who acknowledge their past bad decisions, express remorse, and show that they're determined to work toward redemption.

SELF-DIRECTED QUESTIONS:

In the pages to follow, to complete a self-directed exercise, write your responses to the following three questions.

1. Who are your avatars, and how do they relate to the success you want to build?
2. What would they expect of you?
3. In what ways are the decisions you're making today leading you closer to earning support tomorrow?

VALUES / GOALS / ATTITUDE / ASPIRATION / ACTION / ACCOUNTABILITY

7. Real Estate
USING CREATIVE FINANCING TO GROW

Discussing the pathway to purchase our first appreciating asset in an appreciating market, even though we did not qualify for conventional financing after my release from prison.

Serving time in prison doesn't mean that society has completely abandoned us. While serving my sentence, I would not allow the walls or boundaries to serve as an excuse for my responsibility to understand what's happening in the world. Like almost everyone in prison, I expected to return to society. With that expectation, I always felt an urgency to expand my awareness of the broader community. That understanding would lead to better planning for ways that I could add value or triumph over obstacles.

During my final years inside, I read articles describing the economic recession. In 2008 the stock market and the real estate market began to implode. Credit dried up. Housing prices in many parts of the country dropped by more than 40 percent. Talk radio stations discussed high unemployment rates that led millions of families into hard times. Foreclosures on personal residences and bankruptcies rose to unprecedented heights.

After more than four years of lean times, the economy looked poised to rebound in 2012—the same time I transitioned to the halfway house.

With expectations that the country would pull out of a recession, Carole and I looked for opportunities to participate in the potential upside. We believed that if we could acquire a house at recession-level prices, our equity would grow as prices appreciated.

Since I hadn't finished my obligation to the Bureau of Prisons, rules would preclude me from applying for a traditional mortgage. Further, with a 0-0-0 credit score, I wouldn't qualify. Without access to conventional financing, purchasing a property would require a creative finance strategy. Fortunately, the seeds Carole and I began sowing before my release could help.

What were those seeds?

I can name many, stretching back to the time that authorities locked me in the Pierce County Jail while I awaited sentencing. Throughout the entire journey, I worked to build a record that would show I knew how to:

1. Define success at different stages,
2. Create plans that would lead to incremental steps of success,
3. Put priorities in place,
4. Build tools, tactics, and resources that would advance me along the plan,
5. Develop accountability metrics to measure progress, and
6. Execute the plan daily.

Before my release from prison, Carole and I agreed on a solid plan for how we would build our future together as a team. Since we knew that I'd be starting my career, we intended to count on Carole's earnings as a registered nurse to provide the initial stability for our family. I anticipated that I would need about five years to build a business model that would ultimately sustain us, understanding that I would have to work on many projects without compensation.

I expected to work at least 60 hours each week during my first five years of liberty. If the market required me to travel, I would drive or board a flight and pay for a hotel to seize an opportunity. To earn a living, I would ghostwrite books for others, create products we could sell, or offer mitigation services that our small consulting business could provide to law firms or individual defendants that faced challenges with the criminal justice system.

As Carole and I sat in the prison's visiting room before I transitioned to the halfway house, we discussed my anticipated heavy work schedule. We agreed that it would make sense for her to advance her nursing credentials while I worked to build my career. Carole's research led her to The University of San Francisco's nursing school, where she could earn a master's in nursing while simultaneously earning an income from her work as a registered nurse. As a team, we would both focus on our mutual goals.

Although we anticipated that we'd both earn an income, we knew we would need an investment plan. We were both approaching 50 years old. My lengthy imprisonment meant I hadn't been saving systematically toward retirement. Similarly,

Carole's commitment to supporting me throughout the journey meant that she had sacrificed a career that would allow her to save for retirement.

We had to think creatively.

To solve the problem of retirement preparation, I wanted to buy a house when prices were relatively low in 2012. As the economy improved, we believed the housing market would improve. Owning real estate that appreciated over time could contribute to our preparations for retirement, especially if we could find tenants that would pay rent to live in the property. We anticipated that we could build upon our security by owning assets in appreciating markets.

To buy our first house, we considered our strengths and weaknesses. We didn't have a strong financial statement or credit score, but we had a plan and a history of executing our projects.

Since I had documented my adjustment for decades, I could show a track record. Although I made terrible decisions that sent me to prison, masterminds encouraged me to think about avatars and contemplate what those avatars would expect of me. Those thoughts led to my systematic planning:

1. I created a plan to educate myself, contribute to society, and build a support network.
2. After earning university degrees, I began publishing. Those publishing efforts generated an income that trickled in over the years.
3. Rather than wasting those resources, Carole and I used them judiciously. We invested in her nursing education, and we saved.
4. Those decisions led to approximately $100,000 in savings when I returned to society.
5. We could show how Carole's earnings would increase after she earned her master's degree in nursing.

Our solid plans, backed up by our history of accomplishments, persuaded others to believe in us. Even though we didn't have the conventional track record to qualify for a mortgage, we could find a way to purchase our first property.

CREATIVE FINANCING:

I visited Chris and Seth, partners of Advanced Building Solutions, a premier real estate development company with more than $100 million worth of properties under development. Although I'd never met Chris before my release from prison, my friend Lee could introduce me.

Without a doubt, Chris and Seth were the type of people I had in mind when I thought about avatars. Chris and Seth would want to see a record showing that I was different from the foolish young man who began selling drugs when he was 20. I always believed that my prison adjustment would directly influence my ability to overcome challenges upon release.

When I met with Chris and Seth, I showed them the record of accomplishments I'd worked hard to build. As a published author with academic credentials, and support from Lee, Chris and Seth found it easier to believe in me.

We spoke about a new real estate project they were developing in Petaluma, a quaint city about 40 miles north of San Francisco. Although Chris and Seth hadn't broken ground on the properties when I met with them, they told me that when they finished the development, each house in the development would list for about $400,000.

I wanted to buy one of those houses for Carole and me. Yet we didn't have the financial wherewithal to close the transaction without external financing.

Although an initial assessment of our credit score indicated that we weren't credit-worthy to purchase a house using conventional financing, I asked Chris and Seth to consider the totality of our story. I wanted to persuade the developers why it made sense for them to finance our purchase of one of their properties.

To make my case, I encouraged them to consider what we had accomplished under challenging circumstances, showing them what we'd done in the past and our plans going forward. If they extended us financing for a few years, we would be stronger and likely capable of qualifying for conventional financing. By then, Carole would graduate and increase her earning power. I would finish with my obligation to the Bureau of Prisons and be able to apply for credit. Further, the business I intended to develop would provide me with more earnings.

Despite the perceived weakness of our credit score in the fall of 2012, I made a persuasive case that we would grow financially stronger in years to come.

The developers agreed to finance the purchase of our first house. Since they wouldn't have to pay a commission to a real estate agent, they agreed to give me credit on what the commission would be when I qualified for the mortgage. Further, they told me:

"If you could stay that motivated while going through 25 years in prison, we want you to motivate the other members of our team."

They had five locations where they employed scores of people. They wanted me to speak with the team members at each location and agreed to apply what they deemed fair for a speaking fee toward the purchase price. Those resources would apply toward my down payment once I qualified for the mortgage.

We bought our property for $390,000 in the fall of 2012. The developers agreed to accept a check for $12,000 that they would apply toward my down payment.

Since the Bureau of Prisons wouldn't authorize me to purchase anything on credit, we initially put the house in Carole's name. We planted our stake in the ground, becoming homeowners.

Masterminds have frequently said, "The harder I work, the luckier I become."

Without a doubt, Carole and I were fortunate. Support from people like Chris and Seth, or Lee, allowed us to close our first real estate transaction within days of my transition from prison to a halfway house. By signing that agreement, we controlled an appreciating asset in an appreciating market. As I'll describe in the following chapters, real estate values increased in the San Francisco Bay area in 2013, 2014, and 2015. When those values increased, our equity increased, bringing us more financial stability and opening more opportunities to build prosperity.

If we didn't have support, we would not have been able to purchase that first property. We began sowing seeds for that support decades before launching our plan to invest in real estate. Those earlier decisions gave us the track record we needed when the opportunity surfaced. With that track record, we could persuade others to see us for what we would become.

If you're inside a jail, a prison, or in some other type of struggle, I urge you to recognize the importance of each decision you make. Today's decisions influence opportunities that open later. Consider this lesson with every decision, including:

1. The friends you choose,
2. The activities you pursue, and
3. The books you read.

Every decision comes with opportunity costs. Choose wisely.

SELF-DIRECTED QUESTIONS:

In the pages to follow, to complete a self-directed exercise, write your responses to the following three questions.

1. What thoughts have you given to funding your transition back into society?
2. In what ways have you planned to overcome challenges with your transition into society?
3. How would you describe your preparations to fund your retirement?

8. Support Networks
GATHERING TOOLS AND RESOURCES TO FOSTER SUCCESS

To build relationships with influential people, we need to create strategies that show we're worthy of their time and energy.

Whether we're in prison or we're in society, we must follow the rules. While in the halfway house, regulations required that I show full-time employment and earn a steady paycheck. Since I coordinated all that before I transitioned to the halfway house, my case manager authorized me to get out regularly.

Thanks to my preparations before leaving prison, Lee sponsored me as a friend. He set a schedule for me to work 10—hour shifts, Monday through Saturday. I reported to an office and sat at a desk. Instead of working on tasks for Lee's company, I spent time sowing the seeds to build my business.

Building a business requires us to clarify our vision. We've got to help others understand the problem we're striving to solve and convince people that we're qualified and capable of creating a solution.

When I spoke with Lee about wanting to devote my career to improving the outcomes of America's prison system, he didn't see the vision. He understandably thought that, after 25 years inside, I should try to put the prison years behind me.

In my view, mass incarceration represented one of our time's most significant social injustices. While serving a sentence, I saw the irony of statistics: The longer we expose a person to corrections, the less likely people become to function in society. More than anything else, administrators prioritized the security of the institution. Without access to resources that community members take for granted, people serving sentences had difficulty preparing for success. I aspired to create resources that would help people emerge from prison successfully.

Lee encouraged me to develop a plan that would lead to sustainable revenues. If I didn't build personal stability, he pointed out, I would fail in creating solutions that anyone else could use.

TECHNOLOGY CHALLENGES:

During the first several weeks, I had to familiarize myself with technology. The world had changed during the decades I served. When I went to prison, leaders like Bill Gates projected how technology would change our lives. He built Microsoft to put computers in every home and on every desk. His vision had become a reality long before my release date. We didn't only have computers in every home and on every desk but also in everyone's pockets.

I'd read that people found Apple products more intuitive and easier to learn. With my first weekend pass, Carole and I visited the Apple store in Union Square. I purchased a MacBook Pro laptop and a 27" iMac desktop computer. During those first weeks on the job, I learned the basics of how to use these tools, hoping they would improve my efficiency and help me reach a wider audience.

Books and articles have given me a basic understanding of the internet, search engines, social media, and software applications. Yet once I started working with computers, I realized that I would need to invest hundreds of hours to become proficient. Fortunately, I had Carole to tutor me. When she wasn't on the job nursing at the hospital, she sat beside me at my desk, making herself available to respond to my questions while she worked through her studies. I liked her being close by, always willing to assist when I had questions.

WEBSITES:

When Carole first came into my life, we registered the domain name I would use for my website. She retained a web developer to build a site that would help me memorialize the progress I made through the final decade of my imprisonment. I wrote thousands of articles that Carole published on the site. The website became a central location that would demonstrate my authenticity. Once I got out, I had to learn more about WordPress, the platform for my website.

I wrote a daily journal entry for decades and sent my journals home. Carole published each entry as my "daily log" on the website. I wanted people to see the path, that through hard work, an individual could triumph over prison. I made some critical errors in the beginning. Unfortunately, I lost many records with my decision to switch from one web-hosting company to another. We pay the price for inexperience. Several years passed before I became fluent in WordPress and social media.

BUILDING NETWORKS

Although my time inside didn't open opportunities for hands-on experience with technology or computer networks, I developed other skills. Building support networks, for example, helped me a great deal. I always believed that more opportunities would open upon release if I spent time building robust support networks. That strategy influenced my Socratic questioning, with questions such as:

» What steps could I take today to influence people to believe in me tomorrow?

Those types of questions influenced my adjustment. Accomplishments inside could persuade other people to believe in me. I could leverage those relationships to open new relationships. For example, I wrote earlier about my friendship with Justin. After graduating from USC, Justin built a career as a stockbroker. He made some bad decisions that resulted in his conviction for securities fraud, though Justin's crime didn't characterize his entire life. He'd been successful in society once, and as we built our friendship, I sensed that he would be successful again.

When Justin concluded his obligation to the BOP, he launched a nonprofit that we could use to raise funding. With those funds, we could publish books and courses. Justin then attended schools, workshops, and conferences that exposed him to problems people in underserved communities faced.

Through our work, Justin met others who aspired to make an impact on improving outcomes for people in America's criminal justice system. For example, he connected with Scott Budnick, famous for his role as a Hollywood producer of many blockbuster films, including *The Hangover* series, *Starsky and Hutch*, and other big-budget films. Besides making films, Scott had a genuine interest in juvenile justice. He founded The Anti-Recidivism Coalition (ARC), a nonprofit striving to reduce recidivism.

Soon after I got to the halfway house, Scott invited me to visit him in Hollywood. Rules precluded me from being able to travel until I concluded my obligation to the Bureau of Prisons. My case manager authorized me to leave the halfway house for work six days each week, but he couldn't allow me to travel outside my jurisdiction to Southern California.

Travel limitations and halfway house restrictions presented problems, but human support networks offered solutions. Since I lived in San Francisco, Scott introduced me to Chris Redlitz, a venture capitalist interested in criminal justice reform. Thanks to Scott's introduction, Chris invited me to meet him in Marin.

Chris's firm Transmedia Capital matched investors with technology entrepreneurs who wanted to build compelling businesses that changed the world. Besides offering to fund entrepreneurs, Chris also ran a series of business incubators, providing resources for technology startups.

When not putting multi-million-dollar investments together, he and his wife volunteered at the San Quentin state prison. Initially, he visited the prison to speak about entrepreneurism. The people he met inside inspired him. Chris then went home and convinced his wife and business partner, Beverly Parenti, to join him. Together they launched The Last Mile, an organization that would invest time, energy, and resources to create pathways for people in prison to prepare for success. They created a comprehensive curriculum to teach business principles to people serving sentences at San Quentin. Later, Chris and Beverly grew The Last Mile into one of the most transformational programs in prison—creating programs that would teach people how to code computers.

As I look back, I always see the connections, and I'm grateful:
1. By reading about people like Socrates, Mandela, and Viktor Frankl, I developed hope that a person could lead a life of meaning and relevance after prison.
2. Opportunities to learn existed in every prison.
3. With commitment, a person could learn to read, write, and communicate better.
4. Communicating better could lead to supportive relationships.
5. Through supportive relationships, opportunities would open.
6. That strategy led to a business relationship with Justin, which led to a connection to Scott Budnick and an introduction to Chris Redlitz.

Through Chris Redlitz, I met Tulio Cardozo. Tulio was one of the first graduates of The Last Mile. As I had done, Tulio made some bad decisions as a young man, becoming involved with drugs. While incarcerated, however, Tulio chose to reinvent himself. Through textbooks, he trained himself how to code computers while he served his sentence at San Quentin. Those efforts brought Tulio to the attention of Chris Redlitz, and Chris authorized Tulio to participate in The Last Mile training program. When Tulio concluded his prison sentence at San Quentin, Chris offered Tulio an internship. In that role, he learned more about working with technology companies.

As it turns out, Tulio also followed the pattern of masterminds. He lived deliberately, and his actions led to success.

Although I didn't know much about technology, Tulio had a wealth of information. He invested hundreds of hours helping me to understand the internet and how to use technology. Whenever I had a technology problem, Tulio stood by, ready to offer guidance and a helping hand. If he didn't know how to solve the problem, he used his resources to help me find solutions. Human connections proved incredibly valuable in accelerating growth.

1. What type of human connections are you making?
2. What could you do today to build stronger, more valuable relationships tomorrow?
3. In what ways will the bonds you build contribute to your success?

QUORA:

Besides introducing me to Tulio, Chris Redlitz also introduced me to the importance of social media. Historically, prisons isolate people inside from the broader population. Yet Chris recognized that if people were going to overcome the challenges they would face upon release, they would need to build stronger connections. Although people in prison didn't have direct access to the internet, through volunteers, they could use Quora to interact indirectly.

As a question-based website, Quora invites others to share their knowledge with the world. Anyone with access to the internet could use Quora to ask questions or offer responses. Those who responded with subject-matter expertise received more attention. When people asked about prison on the website, The Last Mile team would print those questions and bring them to San Quentin. Men who participated in The Last Mile program had subject-matter expertise on such topics and handwrote responses to questions that people asked. Volunteers from The Last Mile converted the handwritten responses into a digital file and published responses on the Quora website.

"You should open a profile on Quora," Chris advised me during our first meeting. "Start answering questions about prison."

When I returned to my computer, I logged into Quora and began to explore. In the search field, I typed prisons and saw all types of questions. I started to answer, always being authentic about my experience. Responses I wrote generated more than 1 million views, broadening my social network. Later, I had an opportunity to visit the Quora headquarters and meet team members who built the network.

That exposure to my writing opened many opportunities to advance the career I aspired to build. Editors of other publications contacted me and asked permission to republish more of my writing. Gizmodo, a popular technology website, published one of my articles, generating thousands of new connections. An editor from The Daily Dot, another online news service, invited me to contribute articles. I received invitations to contribute articles for many publications, and the publicity brought me to the attention of a professor at the University of California in Berkeley.

"I've got more than 700 students who want you to come speak about your experiences in prison," Professor Ross said.

I'm hoping that readers in jails or prisons will see the pattern. Opportunities opened when I transitioned from Atwater to the halfway house in San Francisco. But had I not prepared myself during the decades I served, none of those opportunities would've opened.

When my sentence began, I didn't have any academic credentials and didn't know how to write a coherent sentence. I certainly couldn't stand in front of large audiences and give a one-hour speech or write for publication. Exposure to Socrates taught me the art of Socratic questioning.

Instead of focusing on my struggles, I focused on what my avatars would expect. By anticipating their expectations, I had reason to avoid negativity and criminal influences. Instead, I focused on educating myself, contributing to society, and building strong support networks. Those decisions led to new relationships and opportunities. They empowered me through the time I served and eased my adjustment upon release.

If you're in a challenging situation, look around. Determine whether it makes sense to network with the people around you or whether you should work to connect with people you want to meet in the future.

SOCIAL NETWORKS:

In the months that followed my release, my social media profile grew. By posting regularly on Facebook, thousands of people 'liked' my public page. On Twitter, my followers grew into the thousands. On LinkedIn, I could build an online resume where anyone could read about my passion for improving the outcomes of our nation's prison system. More than 1,000 people followed my progress through LinkedIn.

By building a more extensive social network, I could claim more authenticity. Instead of hiding from my criminal background, I lived transparently, with every step relating to the successful life I intended to build. Anticipating that others would judge me for the bad decisions I made when I was 20, or the decades I served in prison, I created tools, tactics, and resources. Those resources would influence their judgment. I could populate the record with articles I wrote or presentations I made, influencing others along the way.

By influencing leaders, I could open more opportunities. Some of those opportunities brought financial resources, but many did not. Either way, every investment of time I made to spread awareness about the criminal justice system paid enormous dividends. They brought the experience that I needed, new relationships, and new opportunities to persuade others to assist my transition into society.

The stronger my social network became, the more opportunities opened. While in the halfway house, NBC Bay Area Proud profiled my work, PBS NewsHour featured me on a segment, and organizers of a TEDx conference in Silicon

Valley invited me to present. That exposure led to more credibility. I leveraged credibility to further my quest to improve the outcomes of our nation's criminal justice system while simultaneously working to build a career.

SELF-DIRECTED QUESTIONS:

In the pages to follow, to complete a self-directed exercise, write your responses to the following three questions.

1. What efforts have you made to broaden your support network?
2. In what ways do you value the support network you're building?
3. How does your support network influence your daily adjustment?

9. Success after Prison

COLLABORATING WITH LEADERS

To change the criminal justice system, we need to create more alliances with like-minded people. Chapter 9 of Success after Prison reveals the path I took to build collaborations.

SAN FRANCISCO STATE UNIVERSITY:

Improving the outcomes of America's criminal justice system would require a significant investment in advocacy. In my view, those changes would require a multi-pronged approach to reach many people, including:

1. **Citizens**: The citizens in our country paid the taxes that supported all government agencies. Those citizens wanted community safety but didn't fully understand what happened after a judge sentenced a person to prison. To improve outcomes of the prison system, we would need reforms. Those reforms would be more likely if citizens supported the initiative. With social media, I hoped to help taxpayers understand why it would be in society's best interest to offer more mechanisms allowing people in prison to work toward earning freedom.

2. **Legislators**: Voters elected officials that would represent them in Congress. Those members of Congress would deliberate changes they could make to improve outcomes for all citizens. We needed changes that would incentivize people in prison to work toward earning freedom. Those incentives should lead people to work toward reconciling with society and making amends for the laws they broke. If the people in prison made progress, reforms would allow them to earn incrementally higher levels of liberty.

3. **Practitioners**: People who build careers working in the prison system influence whether programs succeed or fail. If people working in prisons define success on the job as protecting security of the institution, they strive to control every aspect of the prison. That would include what a person reads, who

a person visits, and how a person lives. An overemphasis on security can translate to obstructing people who want to work toward reconciling with society, making amends, or preparing for success after prison. To change the culture of prisons, we need to influence how people who work in prisons think about the people serving sentences.

4. **People**: People serving sentences get bad messaging while they're inside. Policies within the system suggest no path to redemption exists and that society does not welcome people convicted of breaking laws. Other people in prison adapt to that culture, sending a message that the best way to serve a sentence is to forget about the world outside and focus on getting through the sentence. This mindset leads people to adjust to the culture of confinement rather than preparing for success upon release.

To make a change within the system, I would need to build tools, tactics, and resources to reach each of those populations. With social media, I worked to reach citizens in the broader community. Yet effective advocacy meant I would also need to influence people working within the system and those who legislated laws that led to funding the system.

Knowing the influence of academia, I began writing unsolicited letters to university professors within driving distance of the San Francisco Bay, from Sacramento to Silicon Valley. I wanted them to know of my commitment to working toward making a change. By broadening my reach, I hoped to have a more significant influence on helping people understand how we could work toward improving outcomes for all stakeholders of the criminal justice system. Those stakeholders included every citizen in society, those who worked in prisons, and those who served prison sentences.

If the university professors thought it would be helpful, I offered to visit and provide students with the perspective of a person who served time. Many students who majored in criminal justice wanted to pursue careers in corrections, probation, or other law enforcement professions. I knew the students would've read many theoretical textbooks on corrections or different sociological theories. Listening to someone who could share first-hand experiences might contribute to their educational experience.

Dr. Jeffrey Snipes, from San Francisco State University (SFSU), responded to my letter. He led the criminal justice department at SFSU and invited me to visit

the university. Jeff's email encouraged me. As of 2013, I'd never stepped foot on a university campus. I looked forward to meeting Jeff and experiencing a university campus for the first time. My case manager at the halfway house authorized a pass for me to visit the campus.

When I visited SFSU for the first time, I could appreciate more fully how much the bad decisions of my youth had cost me. The crimes I committed led to my separation from society for multiple decades. Still, I believed it was never too early and never too late to begin contributing to making things right. The thousands of students walking around the campus had so much promise. Many of them would go on to do great things in society. I felt grateful to be in their midst.

I met Jeff and his colleagues in one of the university's small conference rooms. They listened as I told them my story for about an hour. Following my presentation, Jeff surprised me. He asked if I would like to work at SFSU. I didn't quite get his question. I went to the campus with thoughts about contributing as a guest speaker. Instead, he asked if I wanted a job.

During my presentation, I told Jeff about my entire journey, including my obligation to the halfway house. For that reason, when he asked if I wanted a job, I assumed he was trying to do me a solid, offering me a position in maintenance or something like that would allow me to accumulate hours. Jeff surprised me when he clarified the offer, saying he wanted me to become a part of the faculty.

Universities had a considerable influence on my adjustment while I served my sentence. Despite not experiencing life on campus, university professors gave me enormous hope ever since I enrolled in my first undergraduate course at the start of my term. When Jeff offered me the teaching position, I sensed an opportunity to expand my mission. When I asked what prompted him to offer the job, he told me he'd known of my work for over a decade. As a graduate student, he said, his professor assigned books I wrote as required reading.

I consider it essential to share that message with people in prison. The decisions they make every day can have an enormous influence on their prospects for success in the months, years, and decades to follow. I didn't know Dr. Jeffrey Snipes while I served my sentence. Nor did I know anyone at San Francisco State University. Yet by writing books while I served my sentence, I sowed seeds for the future. They led to connections that I didn't even know existed.

People in prison should always think about the relationship between today's decisions and tomorrow's opportunities.

After accepting Jeff's offer, I began laying out the course I would teach. He authorized me to design any type of course that would relate to my journey. I created a course called The Architecture of Incarceration and agreed to begin teaching in August 2013. Less than three weeks after finishing my obligation to the Bureau of Prisons, SFSU students would address me as a professor.

I spent hundreds of hours preparing for the semester. Although my job only required me to teach 30 students, I accepted any student who wanted to enroll. Teaching opened opportunities to influence people who would devote their careers to criminal justice, and I wanted to serve them well.

In designing the course, I set a goal of helping the students understand the influences that led to our nation's massive prison system. We incarcerated more people per capita than any nation on earth. I wanted those students to understand that the US didn't always have the world's largest prison population. Our commitment to mass incarceration didn't begin until the early 1970s, accelerating around the time that I began serving time—when President Reagan launched the War on Drugs. I wanted students in my class to understand how we "architected" the pathway to mass incarceration and to know what we could do better.

To begin the class, I told the students about my history of selling cocaine as a young man and about my transformation while serving 26 years. They were somewhat shocked when I revealed my past. As part of the course, I assigned two books I authored during my confinement, including *Inside: Life Behind Bars in America* and *Earning Freedom: Conquering a 45-Year Prison Term*.

Although students referred to me as "professor," I urged them to call me Michael, reminding them that I'd finished serving a prison term only a few weeks before the semester began. We spent our first class going over my complete history. I encouraged them to ask anything about my past, prison experience, or my expectations about life upon release. Each class lasted nearly three hours, and I pledged to be 100% authentic with them.

During the second class, we discussed the evolution of punishment in Western civilization. Before the 18th century, I pointed out, we didn't use prisons or confinement as a punishment. Instead, we only used confinement as a kind of placeholder until after the trial that would determine guilt.

After determining guilt, judges would punish the offender with mutilation or death. The justice administrators would behead convicted felons or rip apart their bodies in grotesque ways, including "drawing and quartering." Such punishment would send four horses running in different directions while strong ropes ripped limbs off the torso of the offenders.

I designed the third class to teach students about evolutions in criminal justice during the 18th century. Scholars referred to that era as "The Enlightenment," a time when people had more hope. Two philosophers, Thomas Hobbes and John Locke presented different theories on human behavior.

According to Thomas Hobbes' view, people were beasts by nature. Hobbes' theory held that people would only refrain from breaking laws if the state maintained a severe penal system that would punish wrongdoing. On the other hand, John Locke believed that all people came into the world with a blank slate—meaning they were neither good nor bad. According to Locke, we all learn behavior through our observations and experiences. People may have learned behaviors that led to criminal actions, but they could also "unlearn" those behaviors and become good.

Those types of philosophical questions, I explained to the students, led other philosophers to question the way we responded to criminal behavior. Instead of responding to every offense with corporal punishment, many people began to propose different ideas.

During the Enlightenment Era, the prison movement began. Instead of using jails as placeholders for people until after the conviction, when authorities could carry out corporal punishment, we began to use confinement as a form of punishment. Rather than punishing the body, we would extract time from people by forcing them to stay locked in a cell for the duration of the sentence.

In the following class, I invited the students to assess the evolution of justice using a scale of one to ten:

» How much did society improve justice by switching to confinement from punishing people by cutting off their heads?

Each student agreed that confinement represented a significant improvement—a ten on the scale.

Then I opened discussions about how our system has evolved since the birth of the prison. We spent the remainder of our course discussing how prison systems changed from the 1800s to the modern day.

To help students understand more, I brought many guest speakers into the classroom, including:

» A Los Angeles County Sheriff's deputy,
» The San Francisco Sheriff,
» A federal magistrate judge,
» Probation officers,
» Community activists, and
» Formerly incarcerated people.

Since I couldn't bring my students into the criminal justice system, I did my best to bring the system to them.

I didn't limit my teaching to San Francisco State University. During my first year of liberty, I spoke at universities from New York to Washington state and regularly at universities in the Bay area, including Stanford, UC Berkeley, and the University of San Francisco. I felt passionate about working to help more people understand our nation's criminal justice system and about working to improve the system for all.

As much as I enjoyed teaching, I knew I wouldn't spend my career in the classroom. I couldn't afford it. As an adjunct professor who taught only one class on campus, my pay capped out at less than $12,000 per year. Teaching a few more courses would increase my income, but without a Ph.D., I wouldn't become a full professor or earn a livable wage.

Returning to school to complete my Ph.D. didn't strike me as a viable option. After all, I'd been out of the workforce for longer than 25 years, and I couldn't afford to take another hiatus to study for three to five years to complete a program.

Since I'd committed to Carole, I needed to achieve dual objectives. On the one hand, I wanted to pursue projects that would improve the outcomes of our nation's prison system and resolve one of our time's most significant social injustices. On the other, I wanted to create income opportunities that would allow Carole and me to enjoy financial stability.

While teaching, I simultaneously worked to develop my Straight-A Guide, a framework for using time in prison to prepare for success. It all began under the theory that people in prison would be more receptive to learning from individuals who had transformed their lives while they experienced the prison system.

People serving time could become cynical. They might reject a message from people who don't know the pain of being separated from society. I wanted to reach people serving sentences because they would play an integral role in advancing any prospect for prison reform. If people weren't ready to succeed upon release, then voters would reject any efforts toward the reforms I felt would be necessary to improve the outcomes of the system.

The many books I wrote during my imprisonment shared the lessons I learned from people I called masterminds. In truth, we all face struggles during our life. Many people overcame significant struggles, and I learned from their stories. Other people could learn from those lessons as well. I simply had to put the lessons into a package, and I called that package The Straight-A Guide.

SELF-DIRECTED QUESTIONS:

In the pages to follow, to complete a self-directed exercise, write your responses to the following three questions.

1. In what ways does the behavior of people in prison influence possibilities for prison reform?
2. In what ways has your personal story advanced prospects for prison reform?
3. What tools, tactics, and resources are you creating to prepare for your success upon release?

10. Straight-A Guide
VALUES-BASED, GOAL-ORIENTED ADJUSTMENTING

Justice-impacted people can use the Straight-A Guide as a framework to re-calibrate through tough times, restoring confidence and strength along the way.

The origins of the Straight-A Guide began after a conversation with my friend and mentor, Lee. He frequently visited during the final years I served. While we sat together, I told him about the books that inspired me. After discussing a leadership book that encouraged readers to think about how their decisions would influence their lives in the next ten minutes, ten months, and ten years, Lee tasked me with an assignment.

The author of the book we discussed wrote for CEOs, but anyone could apply the advice to their decision-making process. Lee urged me to develop a similar framework. He recommended that I create a program of my own to build a career around the lessons I learned.

After our visit, I returned to my housing unit, knowing I had a job to complete. By contemplating different ways to deliver the message I wanted to convey, I came up with the Straight-A Guide. I visualized a comprehensive program with workbooks, audio files, and video files that would include ten modules I could expand upon, as follows:

MODULE ONE: USE VALUES TO DEFINE SUCCESS:

Transformation begins when we identify and articulate the values by which we profess to live. When I started writing, I pledged that I would never ask anyone to do anything that I didn't do. At the start of my sentence, I defined success simply: I would emerge from prison with my dignity intact and opportunities to prosper as a law-abiding, contributing citizen. I wanted to walk into any room without fear that people would discriminate against me because of the time that I served.

I taught that introductory lesson through the context of my journey. First, I needed to accept responsibility and let the world know that I wanted to become something more than a person serving a lengthy prison term.

Rather than allowing my past bad decisions to define me, I thought about my avatars. By asking Socratic questions about what they would expect of me, I could describe the values by which I professed to live.

My avatars would expect a person in prison to:

1. Educate himself,
2. Contribute to society, and
3. Build a support network.

Those three principles became the values by which I professed to live. Through the lesson plans I created in the first module, I encouraged participants to identify their values and to think about the success they wanted to build.

MODULE TWO: GOALS

After working through the first module and identifying values, a participant could work through the second module—setting clear goals that align with how a person defined success.

In my case, I wrote that it didn't matter how I defined success. I had to think about the people I wanted to influence—my avatars. What would they expect? Answering such questions required the question approach to learning.

» How would my avatars define whether I succeeded in my pursuit of education?

I anticipated that they would measure education by a college degree.

» How would my avatars define whether I contributed to society?

I anticipated that if I were to publish, they would consider that I had worked to make a quantifiable contribution.

» How would my avatars define whether I had built a support network?

I anticipated that if I persuaded ten people to believe and vouch for me, my avatars would find it easier to accept me.

From that question-based approach, I set the following goals to guide my adjustment through the first decade of my sentence:

1. I would earn a university degree,
2. I would become a published author, and
3. I would find ten people to join my support network.

After showing the pattern that worked for me, lessons in the second module encouraged participants to articulate their goals, making them specific, measurable, action-oriented, realistic, and time-bound, harmonizing with how they defined success.

MODULE THREE: ATTITUDE

Participants who took the time to identify values and goals could embark upon the Straight-A Guide. In the third module, participants would work to assess whether they had the "right" attitude.

» What defines the right attitude?

In the Straight-A Guide, we identified the right attitude as a 100% commitment to success—as the individual's values and goals defined success.

Any of us could pursue a self-directed strategy to assess our level of commitment to succeed. Many people talk about wanting to succeed. Those who achieve the highest levels of success, however, know that they must fully commit to their values and goals.

MODULE FOUR: ASPIRATION

In the fourth module, participants learn the importance of aspiring to their highest potential. They develop habits of visualizing themselves as something more than their past bad decisions or their current circumstances. When people project into the future, they develop perseverance—a virtue they can draw upon while climbing through challenging times. Aspirations help people stick with their plans, even when external forces work against them.

People going through complicated prison terms benefit from examples that profile others who built lives of meaning, relevance, and dignity inside and upon release. When we see that others have overcome the challenges of imprisonment and gone on to build lives of significance, we bolster our confidence that we can do the same.

As I wrote that module, I reflected on the lessons I learned from Nelson Mandela. In his book *A Long Walk to Freedom*, we saw the author's strength. Despite a corrupt system that required him to endure beatings, forced labor, isolation, starvation, and other indignities, Mandela always felt a higher calling. Rather than worrying about his struggles, he devoted his life to helping all people in South Africa. He aspired to live for something more than his own life, and those visions endowed him with the strength and spirit to overcome the injustices perpetrated against him.

Nelson Mandela and others taught us that when we can see what we're going to become, we strengthen our resolve to endure the moment's challenges.

MODULE FIVE: ACTION

The fifth module show participants that nothing great happens without deliberate intentions. Every person who achieves a high level of personal success understands the need to take incremental action steps. There is an old cliché emphasizing that we must crawl before we can walk, and we walk before we can run. While living in challenging times, however, we need reminders of how the seemingly insignificant steps we're taking today open opportunities that we can create or seize later.

While writing that module, I reflected on the many incremental action steps that influenced my journey through prison. In one of the chapters from *Earning Freedom: Conquering a 45-Year Prison Term,* one of the accompanying texts that would go with the course, I revealed the example of how I transitioned from a high-security penitentiary to a lower-security prison.

During my initial meeting with the management team, I asked what I could do to transfer to a prison with less volatility. The unit manager told me that since my judge sentenced me to 45 years, I belonged in high security and wouldn't leave until I finished serving my sentence. Institutions routinely extinguish hope. Fortunately, leaders like Mandela helped me believe I could act in ways to bring incremental changes. To facilitate change:

1. I found a job that would lessen my exposure to volatility, and the job helped me to avoid disciplinary infractions.
2. I opened opportunities to enroll in a university program, and the studies gave me a reason to persevere.
3. I developed friendships with mentors who collaborated with me to help me become a published author.
4. Writing further my strategy of bringing more influential people into my support network, and they helped me overcome challenges.

All those little steps worked together. My actions led to an outcome that differed from what most people would project for a person who served a quarter century. Over time, I transitioned to prisons of decreasing security, and in each one, I opened more opportunities that would not have been available had I not taken the little steps. Once I got out, I had the resources I needed to integrate with society easily.

Leaders show us that the little steps we take each day put us on a pathway to higher levels of opportunity in the weeks, months, and years ahead.

MODULE SIX: ACCOUNTABILITY

To live as the CEO of our life, we must be intentional about the progress we're making. Instead of waiting for external forces—like the system—to track our progress, we need to create accountability metrics that help us stay the course. Our accountability tools help us figure out ways to measure incremental progress. Leaders teach us that if we anticipate having to pass through decades before release, we must hold ourselves accountable, adjusting along the way.

In retrospect, I could see similarities between what I read about building a business and building an intentional life. People who build businesses follow a path that only they can see. They identify a problem they want to resolve and engineer the tiny steps they must take along the way. Each stage has a specific timeline and requires limited resources. The leaders may reach their goal within the timeline, using the budgets they set or don't. Successful leaders don't make excuses when they fail to achieve their goals. They adjust. To stay on track, they created accountability tools.

Leaders don't wait for external forces to determine whether they're succeeding. They define success, and they hold themselves 100% accountable along the way.

In the sixth module of the course, we encourage participants to develop accountability metrics. If we know what we want to achieve in ten years, then we should be able to reverse engineer the incremental progress we should make.

1. Where should we be in five years?
2. What incremental stage of success should we reach within three years?
3. Since we know the level of growth we should make in three years, we know what we must achieve each month of the current year.

Our accountability metrics keep us on track, helping us assess progress through each month, each week, and each day. If obstacles surface, we adjust.

MODULE SEVEN: AWARENESS

Module seven shows participants how to grasp the importance of keeping our heads in the game. We've got to stay aware of opportunities. When we focus on opportunities rather than obstacles, we always perceive how we can squeeze the most value from each day.

We're aware, alert, and ready to put ourselves on the pathway to success.

We build strength when we understand how tiny steps lead to new opportunities. Others become aware of our commitment, making it more likely for them to collaborate or invest in our progress.

We become aware of opportunities. By creating or seizing opportunities, others become aware of us.

In his book *Good to Great,* the author Jim Collins wrote about the difficulty of getting anything started. Every goal worth achieving requires effort. In the beginning, the endeavor may be exhausting and all-consuming. Over time, however, if we stay the course, our projects develop momentum. To build something great, we must remain alert and aware and constantly invest in development. His book shows that we can reach our highest potential when we apply ourselves with 100% commitment. Although the author wrote about building great companies, those same principles apply to building extraordinary lives. We've got to keep our heads in the game.

MODULE EIGHT: AUTHENTICITY

People with criminal records may face more challenges than those who do not have criminal records. Rather than fooling ourselves into believing those challenges don't exist, we should develop a response. For that reason, module eight covers the importance of building a record of authenticity.

It isn't enough to say we want to succeed. We need plans to convert our adversaries into advocates. From other leaders, I learned that we advance our credibility— or authenticity—when we show how intentional we are with our systemic approach to succeed:

1. We need to be clear about what we're striving to resolve,
2. We need to identify the plan that we're going to use,
3. We need to put priorities in place,
4. We need to build the tools, tactics, and resources that accelerate our path,
5. We need to show how we adjust when necessary,
6. We need to execute our plan day after day.

People who pursue this path put themselves in a better position to convert adversaries into advocates. Through the course itself, people should see authenticity in action.

MODULE NINE: ACHIEVEMENT

Since people frequently spend years in custody before the system grants them liberty, we offer suggestions in module nine to show the importance of celebrating incremental achievements.

The books accompanying our Straight-A Guide course show the different ways that celebrating small achievements empowered me, while months turned into years and years turned into decades. Although we cannot control release dates directly, we can always control our behavior and our preparations for success. Every small achievement should influence possibilities for new opportunities.

The Straight-A Guide shows participants that by following this values-based, goal-oriented strategy, we restore confidence and meaning in our life. We create higher levels of liberty and strengthen our mindset, knowing that we're making daily progress, regardless of external forces or influences.

MODULE TEN: APPRECIATION

In our final module of the Straight-A Guide, we show how we can bring more abundance into our life when we live in a state of gratitude. We grow stronger by expressing appreciation for the blessings that come our way. The pains of confinement lessen when we're working to build a better community for all.

I created a resource by writing the Straight-A Guide during the final months of my imprisonment. I could use the resource to put lessons from Socrates, the Bible, Nelson Mandela, Viktor Frankl, Mahatma Gandhi, and others into a context that would relate to justice-impacted people. They could use it at every stage of the journey. Through the work ahead, I hoped to disseminate the Straight-A Guide to people in jails and prisons across America.

Teaching at San Francisco State University allowed me to influence future leaders of the correctional system. With the ten modules of the Straight-A Guide, I could work to share self-directed strategies with millions of justice-impacted people. Together, we could collaborate in ways to improve outcomes for the system.

SELF-DIRECTED QUESTIONS:

In the pages to follow, to complete a self-directed exercise, write your responses to the following three questions.

1. In what ways are you using a step-by-step plan to reach your highest potential?
2. How would you create a framework to share ideas with others?
3. How can you influence stakeholders on the need to reform our nation's prison system?

11. Finding Markets

PERSUADING STAKEHOLDERS TO BELIEVE

To lay persuade stakeholders that the Straight-A Guide course could improve outcomes of the criminal justice, I developed a multi-pronged strategy.

Like anyone starting a new venture, I had to overcome many hurdles to convert the Straight-A Guide into a viable, marketable resource. First, I had to consider the potential markets. In my view, those markets included jails, prisons, and schools that served people at risk of going into jails or prisons.

How could I reach people in those markets?

With only 365 days in a year, I had to consider the many limitations that follow for a person getting out of prison. I contemplated such challenges during my sentence, especially as I moved closer to my release date.

As an exercise in personal development, other justice-impacted people can do the same. For example, imagine that you wanted to leave prison with a book or course that you could sell to administrators:

1. What would be the best way to convert the words you wrote into a product that institutions in the market would purchase?
2. How much would you need to invest to create each product?
3. How much would institutions pay for the product?
4. How much would you invest in converting a prospective institution into a client?
5. What would be the difference between the amount institutions would pay and the amount it costs to produce the product?
6. What fixed costs would you need to cover to create each product?
7. What variable costs would you have to pay to make each product?
8. How many clients would you need to build a career around your message?
9. What opportunity costs would you miss if you pursued this path full-time?

10. How could you sustain your family while simultaneously striving to build this venture?

The more questions I considered, the more I realized how complicated it would be to convert ideas into sustainable businesses.

Since I had only recently concluded a long term and still had time to serve on Supervised Release, Parole, and Special Parole, I faced skepticism from many decision-makers. They perceived risk in doing business with me or even allowing me to visit an institution. Still, my commitment to improving outcomes for justice-impacted people kept me pushing forward.

If I could reach people in prison, I believed I could help them see a different path than the one many followed. I wanted to show how disciplined and deliberate adjustment strategies lead to resources they can leverage. Rather than waiting for calendar pages to turn or engaging in the types of thoughtless behavior that derails prospects for success, participants would:

» Find mentors,
» Create opportunities,
» Educate themselves,
» Build strong support networks and confidence in their ability to thrive as law-abiding, contributing citizens.

Yet when making this presentation to people who built careers in corrections, I'd frequently encounter resistance. Many administrators wanted to see independent scholarly research showing evidence that the Straight-A Guide lowered recidivism rates. To provide the proof, I'd need to:

1. Contract with either a research institution or a university research department,
2. Coordinate funding to pay for that research,
3. Find an institution that would allow us to test the course's efficacy,
4. Assess the progress of each participant,
5. Measure the progress the participants made after they returned to society,
6. Compare the success rate of participants who completed the Straight-A Guide with rates of similarly situated people who did not access the program,
7. Coordinate an evaluation with an accredited researcher.

If the independent researchers had access to data, and their research revealed that participants in the Straight-A Guide program were more likely to succeed upon release, we would have more ammunition to distribute the program to jails, prisons, and schools across the nation.

» How much would I have to invest in proving the model?

Although I didn't have first-hand knowledge of budgets, I read that the corrections industry consumed more than $80 billion yearly. Most of those resources went to funding staff and institutions. I didn't know how much administrators would allocate for reentry programs. Further, I didn't have any way of knowing whether working on this project full-time would allow me to earn a living.

Either way, I felt passionate about wanting to contribute.

Mahatma Gandhi advised that we all should strive to live as the change we want to see in the world. By sharing lessons that leaders taught me, I hoped to improve outcomes for other justice-impacted people. In many ways, it was like a calling or a personal ministry. A person who served multiple decades may feel inspired to share lessons that can help other justice-impacted people find their way.

Persistence opened a few opportunities to work with institutions. Slowly but surely, the word spread on how our program helped people build intrinsic motivation. We opened relationships with:

1. Washington State's Prison System,
2. Santa Clara County's juvenile justice program,
3. The City of San Jose's gang-prevention unit,
4. Orange County School District,
5. Los Angeles County Office of Education,
6. Orange County Department of Education, and
7. The Los Angeles County Sheriff's Department.

Revenues from those orders did not cover my production costs, but my relationships with institutions allowed me to interact with thousands of imprisoned people. As time passed, I learned how much I didn't know about the expenses of launching a start-up venture.

Financial resources would have helped, though funding wasn't the driver of my commitment. I wanted to change outcomes for people that went through corrections. To reach that goal, I would need financial stability.

BUILDING FINANCIAL STABILITY:

When I concluded my obligation to the Bureau of Prisons in August of 2013, both Carole and I were 49 years old. We had made progress during our first decade of marriage, but we would have to cover a lot of ground to prepare for a stable future. Carole sacrificed a great deal to marry me, and I promised to work toward stability for our family.

While she advanced toward her master's degree in nursing, I had to earn a living. The values-based, goal-oriented principles of the Straight-A Guide implied that we should never ask anyone to do anything we're not willing to do ourselves. Accordingly, I began asking a series of questions. Since the course urged people to start by defining success, I had to be clear about what I wanted.

When contemplating a definition of success, I had to think about what my avatars would expect. I wanted to connect and influence more law-abiding, tax-paying Americans. To persuade those people that I had value and wasn't only a person with a lengthy prison record, I would have to prove worthy of their support. What risks would they face in befriending me? I bore the responsibility of overcoming their fears or concerns.

Too many people emerged from prison and then reverted to crime. I knew many law-abiding citizens could be cynical about doing business with a man who had served multiple decades. I needed to begin with questions about their concerns, then build credentials to persuade others of my authenticity. They would have to differentiate me from people who talked but failed to produce. Thinking about those avatars would guide my decisions.

In addition to those avatars, I also considered the people in prison I aspired to teach.

1. What would they expect if I asked for their time and attention?
2. How could I earn their trust as someone who could teach them?

3. What could I do to show people in prison that a better life awaited if they would use their time inside wisely?

Answering those questions led me to a conclusion. If I could build a financial statement showing a net worth of $1,000,000, others would deem me successful. I wasn't living an extravagant life and didn't intend to blow money. Yet since my avatars would equate financial success with personal success, I set a goal to make success self-evident.

With that end in mind, I set a goal of building a $1,000,000 net worth within my first five years of liberty. To achieve that goal, I had until August 2018. By succeeding, I would find it easier to inspire more people to see the value of The Straight-A Guide—with or without a validated research instrument.

Once I completed my obligation to the Bureau of Prisons, I could apply for credit. Despite a 0-0-0 credit score, I applied with Bank of America for a credit card. Soon after submitting my application, a banker called, saying she had reviewed my credit application. She had questions. By living frugally and saving resources that our work generated, the combined balances in our account exceeded $100,000.

We didn't splurge after my release. Besides purchasing the Apple computers to launch my career, we didn't buy much. I purchased a used Ford vehicle for $4,000, and we saved as much money as possible. The banker who assessed my application reviewed the assets I listed but asked why her records showed a 0-0-0 credit score. She wondered why I didn't exist in the credit system.

After telling her my story, she agreed to issue my first credit card. Once I received the credit card, I felt a bit more like a citizen. Soon my credit score rose to the high 600s. The next step would be to apply for permanent financing on the house we purchased.

I had promised Chris and Seth of ABS Development that I would pay off the balance we owed on the property as soon as I could qualify for a mortgage. We had signed an agreement with them to purchase the property in the fall of 2012 while I was still in the halfway house. To help us get established, they accepted our down payment of $12,000 and agreed to accept interest-only payments on the outstanding balance until we could pay off the note. We were ready to begin the process of getting our first mortgage.

FIRST MORTGAGE

Carole and I met with a mortgage banker and provided all the requested documentation. We took the next step of ordering an appraisal of the property. Considering comparable prices in the neighborhood, the appraiser provided documentation valuing our property at $442,500.

To avoid additional charges for mortgage insurance, we agreed to accept a mortgage of 80% of our home's appraised value, or roughly $354,000. We wrote a check to cover the remaining amount we would owe to pay off the note to ABS Development.

With the initial $12,000 down payment and the additional funding we had to pay when we closed escrow, our total out-of-pocket investment in the property was less than $40,000. But in less than 18 months of ownership, our total equity in the property surpassed $88,000—or more than twice what we invested.

In applying for the mortgage, Carole and I considered the term of the loan. Traditionally, most people finance their properties over 30 years. The longer amortization brings the advantage of lower monthly payments. With the longer term, however, payments during the first half of the loan went primarily to satisfy the interest. Since we wanted to build equity in the property at an accelerated rate, we financed it with a schedule to pay the house off in 15 years. The monthly payments would be higher at $2,509, but each payment would reduce our debt on the mortgage by more than $1,500.

The advantage of owning real estate we financed over a 15-year term became readily apparent. Once the housing market started to heat up, our property's higher valuation would increase our equity. If we looked at a five-year plan and property values increased by 20% over that term, our $442,000 property would be worth $530,000. In addition, by making our mortgage payments on time over a five-year period, we would reduce the mortgage debt we owed on the property by at least $100,000. If those plans worked out, we could project equity in the property of more than $250,000 after five years—a great return on the money we invested in purchasing the property.

As I made these projections, it became clear that real estate could and should play a significant role in my plan to build credibility. If I could replicate the strategy a few more times, I would reach the goal of building a $1,000,000 net worth by August of 2018, five years after I concluded my obligation to the Bureau of Prisons. I would only need to make my mortgage payments on time and build my career.

To build my career, however, I would still need to persuade more institutions to purchase The Straight-A Guide. Without independent research to validate the program as being evidence-based, I would continue to meet resistance in the marketplace. Administrators would object, saying that although I used the course to become successful, there was no guarantee that others could do the same.

I needed to build more credibility to overcome administrative objections that I anticipated. One strategy would be to write more, speak more, and create opportunities to put me in front of more prospective buyers. Each of those strategies required financial resources.

Accordingly, I started cold-calling potential sponsors who would want to get on the right side of history. Their funding could lead to reforms that would improve outcomes for justice-impacted people.

SELF-DIRECTED QUESTIONS:

In the pages to follow, to complete a self-directed exercise, write your responses to the following three questions.

1. In what ways does an adjustment through prison influence prospects for successful real estate investments?
2. How could you replicate a strategy of using time in prison to prepare for success after prison?
3. In what ways does the development of communication skills relate to success upon release?

VALUES / GOALS / ATTITUDE / ASPIRATION / ACTION / ACCOUNTABILITY

12. Raising Capital
GENERATING FINANCIAL AND HUMAN RESOURCES TO REACH GOALS

To reach our goals, we need many resources. The relationships we build today can lead us closer to those resources, both financial resources and human resources.

I'm grateful to Plato, the philosopher who lived longer than 2,000 years ago and wrote the story of Socrates. His teachings influenced my thinking and approach to solving problems.

I relied upon a Socratic, question-based approach to learning to figure out the next steps in my career development. The more questions I asked, the more truth I found in the saying:

» The one thing I know is that there is a lot that I don't know.

By spring 2014, I'd been free from the Bureau of Prisons for eight months. By then, I had nearly finished teaching the second semester at San Francisco State University, and I'd become more familiar with the different technology applications, hardware, and software.

Social media helped to spread awareness for the work I was doing, and that awareness opened opportunities. Still, I would need resources to fund airfare, lodging, and local transportation as I traveled to meet with administrators who might consider offering the Straight-A Guide in their institutions.

I crafted a plan, hoping to find ten corporate sponsors who would pledge $10,000 annually for three years. With $100,000 in annual sponsorship, I hoped to work full-time toward creating and distributing courses that would improve outcomes for people in America's criminal justice system.

NEWPORT BEACH:

In my search for corporate sponsorship, I called Andris in the spring of 2013. I met Andris during my final months at the Atwater prison camp. He served a brief sentence for a white-collar crime, and I enjoyed listening to him describe the different businesses he launched before authorities charged him with obstruction of justice.

During his senior year in college, Andris launched Ameridebt, which he described as a debt-consolidation business. As a fee-based service, the business helped consumers renegotiate their debt with credit-card companies—Andris leveraged profits from that venture to launch numerous other ventures.

Andris served time in the federal prison camp at Atwater as an indirect result of a civil investigation. The Federal Trade Commission had sued Andris and the company he founded for deceptive advertising. His settlement agreement with the agency required Andris to cooperate fully with the agency. When he refused, prosecutors brought an obstruction charge. Rather than fighting the case, Andris pleaded guilty, and a federal judge sentenced him to a term that would require him to spend nine months in the Atwater federal prison. Despite that setback, Andris remained optimistic because of a separate property development company that he owned. Based out of Newport Beach, the business generated more than $20 million in annual revenues.

When I called Andris and requested that his business sponsor my efforts, he invited me to visit him in Newport Beach. Since my probation officer had authorized me to travel domestically and to meet with anyone to develop the venture I intended to build, I agreed to book a flight from San Francisco to Orange County. When we met, I told Andris about my ambitions of creating products and services that would improve the outcomes of America's criminal justice system. He listened patiently, and then he asked me a series of questions:

1. "Why would people who operate prisons care whether people inside came out successfully?"
2. "What makes you think administrators would buy products you create?"
3. "How long would it take before you start generating purchase orders?"
4. "Can you build a business around these ideas?"

His questions prompted a lengthy discussion. From Andris's perspective, people didn't care about the prison system or the people serving time. I felt it was my job to change those perceptions. Wanting more people to realize that our nation's commitment to mass incarceration influenced every American citizen, I asked for his help.

"I guess you need to ask yourself a question," he said. "Do you want to change the world, or do you want to make money?"

I thought I could succeed on both fronts, earning a good living while working to empower and inspire others.

"Maybe you can, maybe you can't," he responded. "But you've got a lot of passion for this stuff that no one cares about. If you could translate some of that energy into business, you could come work with me, start making money right now, and build products to change the prison system on the side."

I asked what he had in mind. Andris invited me to join his team as a full-time employee and contribute as needed. Showing he wasn't a guy who made empty offers, he pledged to cover my housing expense for the first year and pay a $100,000 salary while we figured out what I'd do.

What's the lesson here?
Some might say I was lucky. In my view, we create our luck. Had I not sown seeds early during my prison term, Andris would not have believed in me. He wouldn't invest in a person unless that person made a massive investment in "self" first.

» What investment are you making in yourself today?
» What investment can you make in yourself right now that will influence other people to invest in your future?

TRANSFERRING JURISDICTIONS:

Since I hadn't completed my term of Supervised Release when Andris offered the job, moving from San Francisco to Newport Beach would not be easy. Authorities required that I report to a probation officer in the Northern Judicial District of California. Employment with Andris' company would require me to relocate to Orange County and transfer my probation to the Central Judicial District of California.

Besides convincing my probation officer to support my move, I'd have to persuade a probation officer from the Central District to authorize my transfer.

If I could overcome those challenges, I'd have a few additional complications to resolve. Fortunately, the seeds I began sowing at the start of my journey positioned me to seize opportunities like the one Andris offered.

Carole liked the idea of transitioning from working exclusively for the prison industry and pursuing other ventures. The compelling job offer would open new opportunities.

I took the next step of contacting my probation officer. Once the probation officer assured me he would support the move, I told the university that I would not return to teach at SFSU in the fall of 2014. Instead, Carole and I would move to Southern California.

RETURN ON INVESTMENT

A conventional mortgage company gave Carole and me the financing we needed to pay for the house my friends Lee, Seth, and Chris allowed us to purchase. Since acquiring the property in 2012, when I first reported to the halfway house, the housing market in the San Francisco Bay area has skyrocketed. We could've sold the house quickly for a substantial profit.

Feeling that housing prices would continue to rise, Carole and I agreed to hold on to the property. We would find suitable tenants who would rent from us. The rental income we received would allow us to pay the mortgage and keep the property as part of our retirement plan. If all went according to our plan, Carole and I would own the property outright by the time we turned 65. By then, we anticipated the house would be worth more than $1 million. We considered the investment an excellent resource to advance our goals for a stable retirement.

Owning real estate, it would seem, could become an integral component of our plan to build a million-dollar net worth within five years. Carole and I pledged to work together in ways that would position us to acquire more.

ORANGE COUNTY: .

After teaching my final class at SFSU in May of 2014, Carole and I loaded our small, four-cylinder Chevy for the seven-hour drive from San Francisco south to Newport Beach.

Despite our income and accumulated savings, Carole and I lived frugally and didn't splurge on purchases that would likely drop in value—like a luxurious automobile. All our daily decisions come with opportunity costs. Leaders would lose respect for my judgment if I were to splurge on an expensive car before building financial security. I needed to make prudent decisions to generate the support that helped my adjustment.

Both Carole and I pursued long-term stability, and we both worked toward those goals each day. When we left the San Francisco Bay area, we had about $100,000 equity in our house and another $100,000 in savings. We considered ourselves fortunate because my 26-year prison term had ended only ten months previously.

We arrived in Orange County just in time to celebrate Mother's Day with my mom and Grandma.

DIGITAL BUSINESSES:

Andris employed more than 100 people, and I hardly interacted with any of them. He employed marketing people, technology people, and an entire floor of salespeople. They asked me for assistance with writing or editing, but other than that, they left me alone. I had the autonomy to develop new business ideas, which led me to form the business that built our website, branded Prison Professors.

Although prison provided the context of my story, my message centered on overcoming struggles. That message had broad applications. Every individual experiences struggle. Too frequently, those struggles derail an individual's confidence. People who experienced challenges that included financial reversals, divorce, obesity, business, or career complications, lived with misery. If we could create products and services in a digital format, we could build something that scaled.

I considered Andris more of a friend and mentor than an employer.

I used my time in the office to learn how to create resources that would allow me to deliver the message in any format that consumers would want, either text, video, or audio.

To paraphrase the celebrated professional hockey player Wayne Gretzky, I needed to skate to where the puck was going rather than to the puck. From my perspective, the educational market would expand. We could produce digital products less expensively, making them easier to distribute.

I intended to create content that would apply to every citizen who aspired to overcome struggle and reach a higher potential. I'd need to build in stages:

1. I'd need to create an abundance of content that would be freely available.
2. I'd need to create proprietary content that I could sell.
3. I'd need to ensure that anyone who had access to the content would find a powerful and actionable message of personal development.

With a plan in place, I started scouring the internet to learn more about how to create digital products.

PODCASTING:

Research led me to a webinar on podcasting. The platform could allow me to communicate with people through audio—as if I had a private radio station. Anyone with an internet connection would be able to access the recordings.

I needed to understand more about technology platforms, software, and hardware to launch a practical podcast. Rather than diving in blindly, which would likely require hundreds of hours, I spent $2,500 to enroll in a course on podcasting. Through the self-directed course, I learned everything I needed to launch the Prison Professors podcast on iTunes.

The podcast would become a part of my overall strategy to broaden my audience, letting the world know more about the courses I would create. I set a goal of creating new content for an ongoing show that would follow a coherent structure. Each episode would last roughly 20 minutes and adhere to one of three formats:

1. I would share strategies I learned from masterminds who taught me how to overcome struggle.
2. I would interview formerly incarcerated individuals who emerged successfully, and they would discuss how their adjustments inside contributed to their successful transition into society.
3. I would interview business and community leaders, asking them about strategies they used to build successful organizations—and also asking them to offer guidance for people who lived in challenging predicaments. What steps could they take to transition into lives of relevance, meaning, and contribution?

Creating a business around digital products remained the focus, and I intended to use the podcast as an integral component of the strategy.

By the end of 2015, I had recorded more than 200 episodes featuring guests from every sector of society. Several guests described their transformation while in prison. They spoke about how their adjustment patterns led to incredible opportunities upon release. Some guests talked about going to prison with histories of violence and substance abuse. Their transformation inside led to their becoming college graduates. The show featured formerly incarcerated individuals who emerged to become practicing lawyers, authors, and entrepreneurs. The podcast also featured interviews with high-profile community leaders.

Each guest shared the trait of personal leadership. They helped me communicate that it's never too early and never too late to begin sowing seeds for a better life. Their stories show that if we choose to live in the world as it exists rather than as we wish it would be, we can create pathways that lead us to success. That strategy of deliberateness worked for the many formerly incarcerated people I feature on the podcast.

I'm convinced a strategy of deliberateness will work for anyone who chooses to lead a values-based, goal-oriented life.

SELF-DIRECTED QUESTIONS:

In the pages to follow, to complete a self-directed exercise, write your responses to the following three questions.

1. What investment are you making in yourself today?
2. What investment can you make in yourself right now that will influence other people to invest in your future?
3. How would investing thousands of dollars in personal-development courses influence prospects for success?

13. Multiple Revenue Streams
CREATING FINANCIAL PLANS TO REACH YOUR GOALS

Preparing for success upon release requires that we think about all our strengths and weaknesses, as well as the opportunities and threats. What will work best for you?

Leaders taught me that I could advance my prospects for success if I lived in a world of reality rather than a world of fantasy. When authorities took me into custody in 1987, I had to live with the fact that I had made many bad decisions as a young man. While locked in the Pierce County Jail, prayers led me to the story of Socrates. From that story, I learned to think about the avatars that would influence my prospects in the future.

Instead of dwelling on the challenges that my bad decisions created, I had to think about the best possible outcome. With that vision, I could engineer a path that would take me from a jail cell, through multiple decades in prison, and into a life of success upon release.

Like most people, I wish I had made better decisions as a young man. If I'd made better decisions, authorities wouldn't have locked me in jail. But I couldn't deal with the world of wishes. No one advanced a station in life by wishing or complaining.

Instead, we had to act deliberately and intentionally.

Reality required that I make new decisions. By thinking about the future, I realized that if I didn't adjust wisely in prison, I would have difficulty finding employment once I concluded my prison sentence. I accepted that the length of time I expected to serve might make it difficult to find any type of meaningful employment.

Throughout the journey, I contemplated what resources to start my life. If I didn't adjust wisely, I wouldn't have anything when my term ended. I wouldn't have clothes to wear, a car to drive, a savings account, or anything. My prison term and a criminal record would always hang over my head. To lessen my vulnerability to such threats, I created several different income streams to advance our prospects for stability.

FINANCIAL MARKETS:

Those who read *Earning Freedom: Conquering a 45-Year Term* or any of my earlier books will know that the stock market influenced my adjustment through prison. After my release, I wanted to speculate on stocks, but I had priorities. Although trading in stocks opened opportunities to build an additional income stream, there were also inherent risks. I couldn't take those risks until Carole and I had more stability.

Each person should remember the importance of setting priorities. I got that wisdom from a leader who told me: "The right decision at the wrong time is the wrong decision." I understood that a time would come for me to resume investments in the market, but first, I had to grow stronger financially and set priorities with the available resources.

By early 2015, our asset base had grown—the real estate market across the United States had caught fire. Soaring valuations lifted our equity, and within two years, the value of our property had grown to more than $550,000. Our tenants paid their rent on time, and we used those resources to pay our monthly mortgage. Our equity in that property exceeded $200,000.

In addition to the paper equity, by living frugally and saving income that I received from speaking events, consulting, and ghostwriting, we built a high balance in our savings account, boosting our net worth to more than $400,000.

Since I'd set a goal of earning my first million by August 2018, I needed to think prudently about every risk and opportunity. I couldn't dither. With my commitment to building a digital product strategy and the work I had to complete for clients who retained me, I didn't have much non-productive time. I had to create podcasts, write articles, record videos, or learn how to use technology more effectively daily.

To reach my financial goals, I would have to focus on investments that could grow in value without requiring too much time. Rather than needing more income, we needed to own more assets that could grow in value. Saving would not be a prudent strategy to advance our goal of earning our first million.

INVESTMENT REAL ESTATE:

The 0-0-0 credit score I had when I walked out of prison had changed. By paying our mortgage and bills on time each month, I built my score to the mid-700s. With good credit, savings, and tax returns showing an income that put us in the nation's top 5% of earners, we planned to acquire more income-producing real estate.

We considered the pros and cons of investing in real estate. On the plus side, we saw how effectively real estate could advance our net worth. By 2015, we could see that more than half of the equity we had built since my release from prison in 2013 came from our real estate investment. That means we made more money while sleeping than we earned while working. If we had been able to purchase additional properties, each would've appreciated equally in the neighborhood. In other words, if we could have replicated our initial investment five times, we would already have a net worth of more than $1 million.

We wouldn't have had to work any harder. We simply needed to control more appreciating assets in appreciating markets.

Instead of looking at the past and wishing we had purchased more, we chose to act, searching for areas where we could replicate the strategy that had worked so well with our first purchase. Real estate investments offered an excellent opportunity to build financial security.

We contemplated purchasing a house where we could live. Real estate values in the Irvine / Newport Beach / Costa Mesa areas of Southern California had appreciated nearly as much as in San Francisco. Single-family residences in Newport started at $1 million, and in nearby Irvine, prices started in the $750,000 range. We anticipated we could move closer to our goal if we used our savings to purchase additional rental properties outside of Orange County.

SEARCHING FOR OPPORTUNITIES:

Investment properties require us to invest 25% as a down payment, and we finance the remaining 75% with a conventional mortgage. Instead of pursuing monthly cash flow, we would continue to finance on shorter terms that would allow us to pay off debt. If the properties could generate monthly income sufficient to make the mortgage payment, they worked for our plan.

Fortunately, living in prison prepared me to understand the importance of delaying gratification to prepare for success.

Real estate values in the high-desert communities of Victorville, Apple Valley, Adelanto, and Hesperia had yet to recover from the economic recession. For the goals that Carole and I set, those communities offered better upside, with less risk for a downside, than properties in Orange County. With an abundance of properties available, investors could purchase properties that ranged between $150,000 and $300,000. Those properties commanded rents of between $1,200 and $2,000, making them attractive.

I anticipated that in years to come, property valuations in the high desert would increase at a higher proportional rate than properties on the coast.

By purchasing properties for less than $250,000 in the high desert, I anticipated that Carole and I could do well over a five-year time horizon. One key factor for us would be to find tenants who could afford to pay the rent.

With our high-desert strategy, we purchased our second investment property in July 2015. Since we had sufficient savings, we paid for the house with a cashier's check for $160,000 and closed on the property quickly. Our tenants signed a long-term lease, paying us $1,200 per month. On the day we took possession of the property, our tenants gave us a rental check for the first month plus a security deposit, replenishing a portion of our savings.

With the property in our name, we began the lengthy process of applying for a mortgage. The appraisal showed the house had a value of $190,000—giving Carole and me an immediate paper profit of $30,000. While waiting for the mortgage to fund, Carole and I replicated our process. Once the mortgage company funded our loan, providing us with a check for 75% of the appraised value, we used those resources to purchase our third property.

Since I wanted to continue acquiring properties, I asked Lee for a loan that I could use for either down payments or acquisitions. When he agreed, we purchased our fourth property.

Cash flow from our tenants allowed us to service our debt. In December 2015, 28 months after my release from prison, independent appraisals showed that we had a solid real estate portfolio with the following assets:

» The total value of our four properties: $1,130,000
» The entire mortgage debt we owed: $605,000
» Our total equity in real estate: $525,000
» The cumulative monthly rental income: $6,800
» Our cumulative monthly mortgage payments: $5,100
» Cumulative monthly positive cash flow: $1,700

Our mortgage payments would incrementally reduce our debt by nearly $4,000 monthly. If nothing changed, rental income from our tenants would allow us to pay off the properties in total over the next 180 months.

Besides the debt reduction, the $1,700 monthly positive cash flow would accumulate over the 180-month plan. Over time, the positive cash flow would lead to additional savings of $306,000—more than the total amount we invested in acquiring our properties.

With those projections, even if the properties didn't do anything more than hold their value, the tenant income would pay off the debt within 15 years, giving us property equity of $1,130,000. On the other hand, if the properties returned to pre-recession valuations, those properties would be worth more than $2 million.

Carole and I used less than $300,000 of our resources to acquire those assets. Buying real estate would advance our goal of building our first $1 million net worth. Best of all, it would proceed on autopilot while I focused on generating new revenue streams with digital products.

Many factors played into our good fortune, including:
1. Market timing worked in our favor. I got out of prison at the end of the recession. When market prices rose, the value of our assets rose.
2. Access to capital allowed me to continue acquiring properties.
3. We found good tenants that paid their rent on time.

I hope readers will connect the dots to see how carefully laid plans allowed us to create and seize opportunities. Each person should begin sowing seeds today that will bear fruit in the weeks, months, years, and decades ahead.

AWARENESS:

Although our growing portfolio of rental properties served as an integral part of our wealth-accumulation strategy, I remained determined to both build a digital-products business and to work toward creating opportunities to improve the outcome for all justice-impacted people. To succeed, I would use a multi-pronged strategy, including the following:

1. Inspiring people going into the criminal justice system to use their time wisely to prepare for success upon release,
2. Collecting data to show how and why mechanisms to earn freedom would serve the interests of all citizens,
3. Opening relationships with stakeholders of the criminal justice system so that we could introduce our programs to more people in prison,
4. Develop conversations with legislators and prison administrators to influence sentencing laws and prison operations.

To open relationships with more leaders, I accepted 12 speaking assignments in the fall of 2015. Those commitments kept me in different airports every week, with travel to cities between Tacoma and DC to create market awareness.

Some of those speaking events provided memorable experiences. When I made my initial sales call in Washington State, I had an opportunity to build a friendship with the state's prison system directors. Those powerful allies helped my small business grow.

Frequently, administrators told me that only a few people could adjust to a long-term so productively. I disagreed, reminding them of my story. When I began serving my sentence, the prosecutor said that even 300 years of imprisonment would not have been sufficient punishment for my crime. And during my first team meeting, my unit manager predicted that I would serve my entire sentence in high-security prisons.

People may see us one way today, but if we can see a better future, we can work to reconcile and make amends, creating better outcomes. More people would work to prepare for success upon release if administrators showed incentivized them along the way.

Slowly, administrators began to believe. Leaders of prison systems allowed me to start bringing programs into institutions. Those opportunities allowed me to connect with people serving sentences in state and federal prisons across America.

Ironically, a captain in the Bureau of Prisons that once authorized my placement in the Special Housing Unit became one of my biggest advocates, bringing our Preparing for Success after Prison course to federal prisons across America. A US Attorney issued a purchase order for us to create a reentry program for her district. Federal judges purchased our programs. We received contracts to provide our courses to every state prison in California. Further, through our relationship with digital platform companies, we expanded our distribution to jails and prisons, reaching more than 100,000 people daily.

A revenue model didn't always accompany those opportunities, but thanks to other business ventures I initiated, we could celebrate our impact on people's lives. It became our way of being the change we wanted to see in the world. For those results, we're grateful.

FINAL THOUGHTS:

With this book, I wanted to show readers the relationship between decisions in prison and prospects for success upon release. In my case, those decisions didn't advance my release date by a single day. But when I came home, opportunities opened for me to build financial success while simultaneously reaching my goals of helping other people who served time in custody.

I'll continue striving to grow and continue documenting the journey.

I'm encouraging all readers to do the same. Work hard. Educate yourself. Reject the criminal lifestyle and focus on preparing for your success. You, too, will grow through these challenges and emerge successfully.

For those who want more information, please visit our website at PrisonProfessors.com. People in prison who want to share their success may use the following contact information:

Prison Professors
32565 Golden Lantern Street
Box B-1026
Dana Point, CA 92629

Impact@PrisonProfessors.com

Last updated: November 15, 2022

SELF-DIRECTED QUESTIONS:

In the pages to follow, to complete a self-directed exercise, write your responses to the following three questions.

1. What expenses do you anticipate needing to meet upon your return to society?
2. What plan do you have in place to meet the expenses you anticipate upon release?
3. How can you use time inside to prepare for your financial retirement strategy?

Made in the USA
Columbia, SC
21 April 2024

34679140R10111